Reading & Writing
Chichén Itzá

Australia • Brazil • Mexico • Singapore • United Kingdom • United States

NATIONAL GEOGRAPHIC
L E A R N I N G

National Geographic Learning,
a Cengage Company

Reading & Writing, Chichén Itzá

**Laurie Blass, Mari Vargo, Keith S. Folse,
April Muchmore-Vokoun, Elena Vestri**

Publisher: Sherrise Roehr

Executive Editor: Laura LeDréan

Managing Editor: Jennifer Monaghan

Digital Implementation Manager,
Irene Boixareu

Senior Media Researcher: Leila Hishmeh

Director of Global Marketing: Ian Martin

Regional Sales and National Account
Manager: Andrew O'Shea

Content Project Manager: Ruth Moore

Senior Designer: Lisa Trager

Manufacturing Planner: Mary Beth
Hennebury

Composition: Lumina Datamatics

© 2020 Cengage Learning, Inc.

ALL RIGHTS RESERVED. No part of this work covered by the copyright herein
may be reproduced or distributed in any form or by any means, except as
permitted by U.S. copyright law, without the prior written permission of the
copyright owner.

"National Geographic", "National Geographic Society" and the Yellow Border
Design are registered trademarks of the National Geographic Society
® Marcas Registradas

For permission to use material from this text or product,
submit all requests online at **cengage.com/permissions**
Further permissions questions can be emailed to
permissionrequest@cengage.com

Student Edition: Reading & Writing, Chichén Itzá
ISBN-13: 978-0-357-13826-7

National Geographic Learning
20 Channel Center Street
Boston, MA 02210
USA

Locate your local office at **international.cengage.com/region**

Visit National Geographic Learning online at **ELTNGL.com**
Visit our corporate website at **www.cengage.com**

Printed in China
Print Number: 02   Print Year: 2019

PHOTO CREDITS

01 (c) © Juan Pablo de Miguel Moreno/Aurora Photos, **02-03** (c) Malgorzata Brewczyk/Alamy Stock Photo, **05** (t) © Alastair Humphreys, **06** (c) © Alastair Humphreys, **09** (t) © Alastair Humphreys, **12** (br) Peter Phipp/Travelshots.com/Alamy Stock Photo, **12-13** (c) © Cengage Learning, Inc., **13** (tl) David M. Benett/Getty Images, **14** (bc) Tim M/Alamy Stock Photo, **15** (bc) © Sergio Pitamitz/National Geographic Creative, **16** (bc) Robert Harding Picture Library/National Geographic Creative, **20-21:** © MICHAEL NICHOLS/National Geographic Creative, **22:** © Lars Christensen/ Shutterstock.com, **24:** © Henrik Sorensen/Stone/Getty Images, **28:** © Seb Oliver/cultura/Corbis, **29:** © Jose Luis Pelaez Inc/ Blend Images/ Getty Images, **274:** © DESIGN PICS INC/National Geographic Creative, **32:** © Daniel rodriguez/ iStockphoto.com; Left: © rsooll/ Shutterstock. com; Right, **34:** © Ivonne Wierink/Shutterstock.com; Top left: © Micro10x/Shutterstock.com;Top right: © Magicoven/Shutterstock.com; Middle left:© Fabio Alcini/Shutterstock. com; Middle right: © Jiri Hera/Shutterstock.com; Middle left:© Ron Frank/Shutterstock.com; Middle right: © Cultura Creative/Alamy; Bottom left: © Robert Kneschke/Shutterstock.com; Bottom right **39** (c) Jordan Pix/Getty Images, **40** (bc) Science & Society Picture Library/Getty Images, **40** (bl) Apic/Getty Images, **40** (br) Royal Photographic Society/Getty Images, **41** (tl) Andreas Feininger/ Getty Images, **41** (bc) For Alan/Alamy Stock Photo, **41** (tc) Adrian Lyon/Alamy Stock Photo, **43** (t) © Chris Burkard/Massif, **44** (bc) © Chris Burkard/Massif, **47** (t) Frans Lanting/National Geographic Creative, **48** (bc) Brian J. Skerry/National Geographic Creative, **51** (t) © Alexyz3d/ Shutterstock,**51** (bc) © Chris Fallows, Pages **58-59:** ″ John W Banagan/Photographer's Choice/Getty Images, Page **61:** ″ MIKE THEISS/National Geographic Creative Page **66:** Top: ″ iStockphoto.com/Justin Horrocks/jhorrocks; Top middle: ″ Gari Wyn Williams/Alamy; Bottom middle: ″ Ian west/Alamy; Bottom: ″ Krafft/Explorer/Photo Researchers, Inc/Science Source, Page **67:** Top: ″ DESIGN PICS INC/National geographic Creatrive; Bottom: ″ Frans lemmens/Alamy Page **71:** ″ Barry Lewis/Alamy, Page **75:** ″ Ariel Skelley/Blend Images/Getty Images, Page **77:** A.L/shutterstock. com **82-83:** © Sylvain Sonnet/hemis.fr/Getty Images, **84:** © Buena Vista Images/ Lifesize/Getty Images **96:** © DEAN CONGER/National Geographic Creative, **97:** © Ana Menendez/Shutterstock.com, **99:** © Eric Carr/Alamy; Left: © czdast/Shutterstock.com; Right ,**100:** © jeehyun/ Shutterstock.com; Top left: © hartphotography/Shutterstock.com; Top right:© Pawel Gaul/iStockphoto.com;Bottom left: © BMJ/Shutterstock. com; Bottom right, **101:** © lexaarts/Shutterstock.com; Top left: © Narongsak Yaisumlee/Shutterstock.com; Top right: © t3000/iStockphoto.com; Bottom left: © Milkos/Shutterstock.com; Bottom right, **107** (t) © Alastair Humphreys; **110** (tl) Peter Phipp/Travelshots.com/Alamy Stock Photo, (tr) David M. Benett/Getty Image; **113** © Chris Burkard/Massif; **116** (tl) © Alexyz3d/Shutterstock, **51** (tr) © Chris Fallows, **123** (b) © Peter Beck/ Corbis/ Aurora Photos; **125** (t) © elwynn/Shutterstock.com; **127** (t) © Ira Block/National Geographic Creative; **128** (b) © Oote Boe 3/Alamy; **130** b) © Jon Burbank/Alamy.

Scope and Sequence

Unit Title and Theme	Reading Texts and Video	ACADEMIC SKILLS Reading
1 **ADVENTURE** *page 1* ACADEMIC TRACK: Geography	**Reading 1** Adventures Anywhere **VIDEO** Hooked on Adventure **Reading 2** A Movie-Goer's Guide to London	**Focus** Understanding Main Ideas of Paragraphs Predicting, Understanding Details, Understanding Purpose

Unit Title and Theme	Writing	Grammar for Writing
2 **VERBS: PRESENT PROGRESSIVE TENSE** *page 20*	Practicing grammar and vocabulary in model writing Guided writing Writing sentences with context	Present progressive tense Single or double consonant before adding *-ing*

Unit Title and Theme	Reading Texts and Video	ACADEMIC SKILLS Reading
3 **THE VISUAL AGE** *page 39* ACADEMIC TRACK: Technology	**Reading 1** Sharing Success **VIDEO** A Million "Likes" **Reading 2** Is It Real?	**Focus** Identifying Examples Previewing, Understanding the Gist, Understanding Main Ideas and Details

Unit Title and Theme	Writing	Grammar for Writing
4 **DESCRIBING ACTIONS** *page 58*	Writing from picture prompts Writing from scenarios Describing actions	The Present Progressive Tense Verbs in Complex Sentences Adverbs of Manner Prepositional Phrases of Place

Unit Title and Theme	Writing	Grammar for Writing
5 **PREPOSITIONS** *page 82*	Writing about the location of places on a map Writing sentences that start with prepositional phrases Guided writing	Prepositions and prepositional phrases Prepositions of time and place: *at, on, in* Word order: Place and time in the same sentence Word order: Beginning a sentence with a prepositional phrase Common preposition combinations after verbs, adjectives, and nouns

Critical Thinking	Writing	Vocabulary Extension
Focus Applying Ideas Synthesizing, Guessing Meaning from Context	**Language for Writing** Using imperative sentences Using *should / shouldn't* **Writing Goal** Write a walking tour of an area you know well.	**Word Partners** Noun + *trip* **Word Web** Prepositions of place and direction

Building Vocabulary and Spelling	Original Student Writing
Words with the sound of **oy** in **boy**	Writing about people who are doing different things right now

Critical Thinking	Writing	Vocabulary Extension
Focus Applying Advice Evaluating, Guessing Meaning from Context	**Language for Writing** Using infinitives of purpose Using *and, but*, and *or* **Writing Goal** Write about what you use the Internet for	**Word Partners** Verb + *photo* **Word Forms** Nouns and verbs with the same spelling

Building Better Vocabulary	Original Student Writing
Word Associations Using Collocations Parts of Speech	Writing about what is happening in an emergency situation

Building Vocabulary and Spelling	Original Student Writing
Words with the sound of **o** in **hello**	Writing about things tourists can see and do in a city

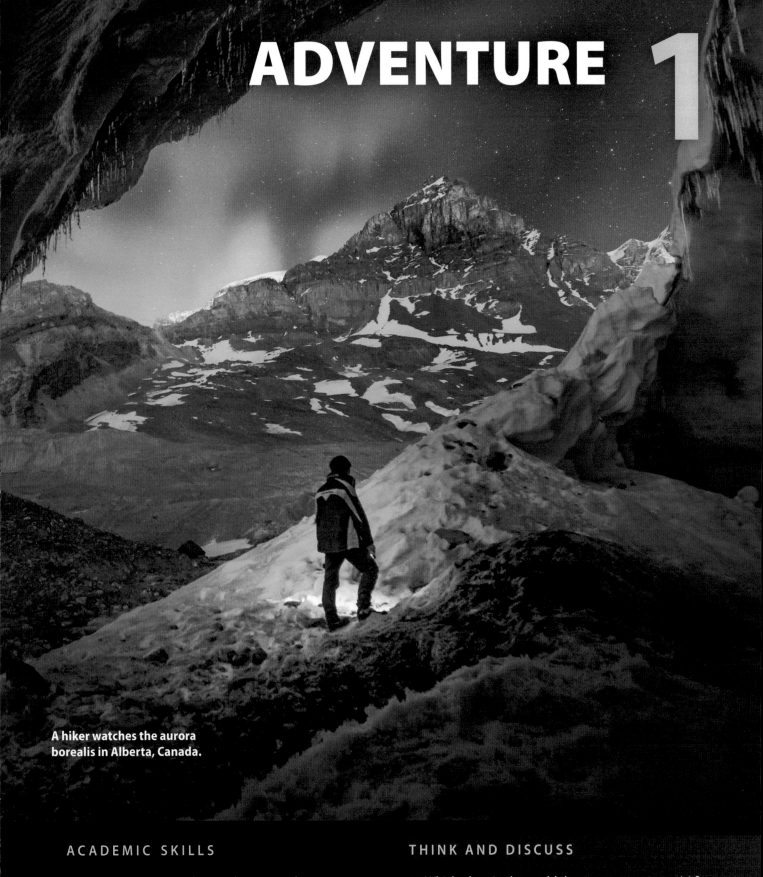

ADVENTURE 1

A hiker watches the aurora borealis in Alberta, Canada.

THINK AND DISCUSS

1 Which place in the world do you most want to visit?
2 What do you want to do there?

A Look at the information on these pages and answer the questions.

1. What age group is this information about?

2. What are three of the places that people in this group want to visit?

B Match the words in **blue** to their definitions.

_____ (n) a journey or vacation

_____ (n) an exciting experience

_____ (v) to decide on the best option

TRAVEL ADVENTURES

Imagine you could go anywhere in the world for a travel adventure. Which place would you choose? A travel company asked this question to 5,500 millennials—people born between the early 1980s and the early 2000s. The ten most popular choices included famous places like the Egyptian pyramids, the Great Wall of China, and the Eiffel Tower. However, number one on the list was a trip to the Blue Lagoon in Iceland.

1. Bathe in the Blue Lagoon, Iceland
2. See the Great Pyramids of Giza
3. Walk the Great Wall of China
4. Relax on Byron Bay beach, Australia
5. Learn how to make pizza in Italy
6. Drive along Route 66, U.S.A.
7. Take a gondola ride in Venice, Italy
8. Climb the Eiffel Tower, Paris
9. Watch sea turtles in Costa Rica
10. Enjoy a picnic in the French countryside

Iceland's Blue Lagoon is naturally heated to around 37–40°C. Iceland has become very popular with tourists in recent years. In 2003, there were around 300,000 foreign visitors to Iceland. By 2016, however, this number was around 1.8 million.

Reading 1 QUICK READ SEE PAGE 106

PREPARING TO READ

SEE PAGE 106

BUILDING VOCABULARY

A The words in blue below are used in the reading passage on pages 5–6. Read the definitions and complete the sentences with the correct form of the words.

> If you go **hiking**, you go on a long—and sometimes difficult—walk in the countryside.
>
> If something is **low-cost**, it is not expensive.
>
> A **map** is a picture of a place that shows roads, mountains, rivers, and other things.
>
> If you travel **across** a place, you go from one side to the other.
>
> **Anywhere** means any place; you say "anywhere" when the place doesn't matter.
>
> If you **climb** something, you go up to the top of it.
>
> If something is **important**, it is special and very useful.

1. When you travel, it is _____ to keep your passport in a safe place.

2. If you go to New York City, you can _____ 354 steps to the top of the Statue of Liberty.

3. You can have a fun adventure almost _____—in a foreign country, in a new city, or even in your hometown.

4. Singapore is a very small country. You can walk _____ it in one day.

5. When you go _____ in a new place, you should take a

   _____ with you so you don't get lost.

6. If you want a(n) _____ vacation, go somewhere in your home country.

USING VOCABULARY

B Note your answers to the questions. Then share your ideas with a partner.

1. What are some good places in your country to go **hiking**?

   _____

2. What are some good **low-cost** vacations that you know about?

   _____

BRAINSTORMING

C What words do you think of when you hear the word *adventure*? Write six words below. Then compare your ideas with a partner.

   _____

PREDICTING

D Read the title and photo caption on page 5. What do you think a "microadventure" is? Discuss with a partner. Check your ideas as you read the passage.

Alastair Humphreys
sleeps on a hill during
a microadventure.

ADVENTURES ANYWHERE

🎧 Track 1

A British adventurer Alastair Humphreys has ridden his bike around the world, walked across India, and rowed from Africa to South America. In 2011, however, Humphreys had some of the biggest adventures of his life—and he never even left the United Kingdom.

B For a year, Humphreys went on microadventures—small, low-cost trips close to home. Why did he do this? "I started to think that it was possible to have an adventure anywhere," he explains. For his first trip, he went hiking with a friend around the M25—a 188-kilometer road that goes all the way around London. Other adventures included swimming in the River Thames, sleeping outside on a hill, and going on a mountain biking trip. Humphreys learned something important from his microadventures: We find adventure when we try something new.

C Humphreys wanted other people to make this discovery, too, so he decided to share his idea. He challenged people to go on microadventures and send him four-minute videos of their trips. He asked them to do things like climb a hill, go away for a weekend, or choose a random place on a map and go there. People from all over the world accepted his challenge and posted their videos on Twitter.

TRY A MICROADVENTURE YOURSELF

Here are six ideas for a microadventure. Why not try one yourself? As Humphreys says, "Life is now or never. Fill it with adventure!"

- Climb a hill that you can see from your town.
- Sleep in your garden for a night.
- Go on a journey to an island.
- Choose a river and travel to where it starts.
- Travel to the coast and sleep there for a night.
- Take a friend on their first microadventure.

"In life it doesn't matter what you do, just that you do something."

Alastair Humphreys

Alastair Humphreys relaxes during a microadventure in the U.K.

UNDERSTANDING THE READING

A What is a microadventure? Check (✓) the best definition.

☐ a. It's a trip you take by yourself.

☐ b. It's an adventure you have in a foreign country.

☐ c. It's a trip close to home that isn't expensive.

B Which of the following are true about Alastair Humphreys? Check (✓) all that apply.

☐ a. He has had amazing adventures in foreign countries.

☐ b. He believes his biggest adventure was rowing across the Atlantic Ocean.

☐ c. He spent a year having adventures in his home country.

☐ d. His first microadventure was swimming in the River Thames.

☐ e. He challenged people to go on microadventures and make videos of them.

C Find and underline the following words in the reading on pages 5–6. Use the context to help you understand the meaning. Then circle the correct options to complete the sentences.

> **rowed** (paragraph A)   **random** (paragraph C)   **accepted** (paragraph C)

1. If an event is random, it **follows / doesn't follow** a plan.
2. You can row a **boat / car**.
3. If you accept a challenge, you **agree / don't agree** to do it.

> **CRITICAL THINKING**   **Applying** means using an idea in a new way. It can help you understand and remember an idea better. For example, applying Humphreys's idea to your own town can help you understand what he means by "microadventure."

D Work with a partner and discuss your answers to the following questions.

1. Look at the microadventures listed on page 6. Which of these microadventures can you do where you live?

2. What are some other microadventures you can have in your area? Note your ideas.

_____

_____

_____

DEVELOPING READING SKILLS

> **READING SKILL** Understanding Main Ideas of Paragraphs
>
> The main idea of a paragraph is the most important thing or idea that the writer is saying. A paragraph usually has one main idea. This idea is often introduced in the first or last sentence of the paragraph.

ANALYZING **A** Read the paragraph and circle the main idea (a–c).

> There aren't many places better than New Zealand for an adventure holiday. You can try almost any kind of adventure sport, such as surfing, white water rafting, and climbing. New Zealand is also famous for bungee-jumping. One of the first bungee-jumping sites in the world opened in the late 1980s at New Zealand's Kawarau Bridge.

a. Most people visit New Zealand to go bungee-jumping.

b. Surfing is one of the most popular sports in New Zealand.

c. New Zealand is a great place to go for an adventure holiday.

UNDERSTANDING MAIN IDEAS OF PARAGRAPHS **B** Look again at paragraphs A, B, and C on page 5. Then circle the main idea for each paragraph.

1. Paragraph A

   a. Humphreys's most enjoyable adventure was walking across India.

   b. Some of Alastair Humphreys's biggest adventures were in his home country.

   c. Alastair Humphreys's biggest challenge was rowing from Africa to South America.

2. Paragraph B

   a. Humphreys went on small adventures near his home for a year.

   b. On his first microadventure, Humphreys learned a lot about his friend.

   c. Humphreys's favorite microadventure was swimming in the Thames.

3. Paragraph C

   a. Other people challenged Humphreys to go on microadventures.

   b. Humphreys went on microadventures with other people.

   c. Humphreys challenged other people to go on microadventures.

UNDERSTANDING MAIN IDEAS OF PARAGRAPHS **C** In which paragraph was the main idea mentioned in the last sentence?

Video

HOOKED ON ADVENTURE

Alastair Humphreys

BEFORE VIEWING

A What do you remember about Alastair Humphreys from the reading on pages 5–6? Note three things you remember about him. Then share your ideas with a partner.

BRAINSTORMING

1. _____

2. _____

3. _____

B Read the sentences. The words in **bold** below are used in the video. Match each word with the correct definition.

VOCABULARY IN CONTEXT

> Sleeping outdoors can be quite **comfortable** if you have a good tent.
>
> Microadventures are easy to do and not expensive, so there's no **excuse** not to try one.
>
> When I was young, I went on a very **memorable** vacation with my grandparents.
>
> Humphreys loves adventure. In fact, he says he's **hooked on** it.

1. _____ (adj) wanting to do something again and again

2. _____ (adj) easy to remember because it is special or fun

3. _____ (n) a reason you give for not doing something

4. _____ (adj) making you feel relaxed

C Read the information about Alastair Humphreys. Then answer the questions.

In August 2001, Alastair Humphreys rode his bicycle 74,000 kilometers around the world. He traveled through 60 countries, and the whole journey took him four years. By the time he got back, Humphreys was hooked on adventure. He went on other amazing journeys and wrote about his experiences. He continues to write, and also works as a speaker, encouraging people to add more adventure to their lives.

1. How was Humphreys's first adventure different from a microadventure?

_____

2. What do you think were Humphreys's biggest challenges on his trip round the world?

_____

WHILE VIEWING

UNDERSTANDING
MAIN IDEAS

A ▶ Watch the video. Check (✓) the microadventures that Humphreys talks about.

☐ a. sleeping on a hill in another city   ☐ b. going on a journey to an island

☐ c. traveling to the coast   ☐ d. climbing a hill with a group of friends

UNDERSTANDING
DETAILS

B ▶ Watch the video again. Answer the questions. Circle the correct option.

1. According to Humphreys, what is the main reason people don't go on adventures?

   a. They think it will be too expensive.

   b. They don't know how to get started.

2. What did Humphreys learn in Hong Kong?

   a. You can have a microadventure even if you live in a big city.

   b. It's important to plan your microadventures carefully.

3. What does Humphreys mean when he says, "Tick-tock, tick-tock, this is our life"?

   a. Life is short, so we should use our time well.

   b. People's lives today are too rushed. We need to relax more.

AFTER VIEWING

CRITICAL THINKING:
SYNTHESIZING

A Think about the microadventures in the video and the ones you read about on pages 5–6. Which microadventure would you most like to go on? Note your ideas below. Then discuss with a partner.

Microadventure: _____

Reason: _____

_____

Reading 2   QUICK READ   SEE PAGE 109

PREPARING TO READ

A Read the information about San Francisco. The words in blue are used in the reading passage on pages 12–13. Match the correct form of each word with its definition.

BUILDING
VOCABULARY

> The best way to see San Francisco is to take a walking **tour**. There are many interesting **locations** you can travel to on foot.
>
> When you are in San Francisco, you should **check out** the **Museum** of Modern Art. It's a great place to see the work of some **amazing** modern artists.
>
> There are always **crowds** in Union Square because people like to shop there. There are also a lot of places to eat **nearby**.
>
> Some people think San Francisco is the **capital** of California, but it's actually Sacramento.

1. _____ (n) the city where the government is located

2. _____ (adj) very good, often in a surprising way

3. _____ (n) a place

4. _____ (n) a building where you can look at interesting objects

5. _____ (adv) very close to a particular place

6. _____ (n) a large group of people

7. _____ (n) a trip to see interesting sights

8. _____ (v) to visit or to look at (something)

B Answer the questions. Then share your ideas with a partner.

USING
VOCABULARY

1. When did you last go on a **tour** of a city? Where did you go? What did you see?

   _____

2. What are the most **amazing** things to see in your country?

   _____

3. When did you last go to a **museum**? What did you see there?

   _____

C You are going to read a passage about a tour of the city of London. What do you know about London? What famous locations are there? Share your ideas with a partner.

BRAINSTORMING

D Read the passage. Are any of the locations you thought of in **C** mentioned?

A MOVIE-GOER'S GUIDE TO LONDON

🎧 Track 2

A London has been the setting[1] for many popular movies—from James Bond to Harry Potter. So if you are visiting the UK's **capital**, why not follow this walking **tour** and explore some interesting movie **locations**?

B Start at ❶ **the London Film Museum**. Here, you can see a collection of items from many famous movies. The **museum** is near Covent Garden—a famous market. And while you're there, you should **check out** some of the **amazing** street performers.

C Next, walk down King Street, then along New Row to ❷ **J Sheekey**. This restaurant is a great place to see TV and movie stars. And it's not too expensive; you can get a great meal for under £25.

D Nearby is ❸ **Leicester Square**, known as London's "Theatreland." Many famous movie premieres[2] are held in the square, and it is also home to the London Film Festival. One of the exits of the Leicester Square underground station appears in the movie *Harry Potter and the Half-Blood Prince*.

E To get away from the **crowds**, you should spend some time in ❹ **Leicester Square Gardens**. Here, you'll see a statue of William Shakespeare. Shakespeare wrote his most famous plays while he was living in London. Many of his plays, such as *Macbeth*, were later made into movies.

F From Leicester Square, walk down to Charing Cross Road and then to ❺ **the National Gallery**. Here, you can see famous paintings by artists like Vincent van Gogh and Leonardo da Vinci. This museum was also a location in the James Bond movie *Skyfall*.

G Finally, go south on Charing Cross Road, past the underground station—which appears in *Thor: The Dark World*—and follow the Mall. At the end of the Mall, you'll see ❻ **Buckingham Palace**, the home of the British royal family. The palace appears in several movies, such as *The BFG* and *The King's Speech*.

Guards march outside Buckingham Palace.

[1]**setting:** the place or area where an event takes place
[2]**premiere:** the first performance of a play or the first showing of a movie

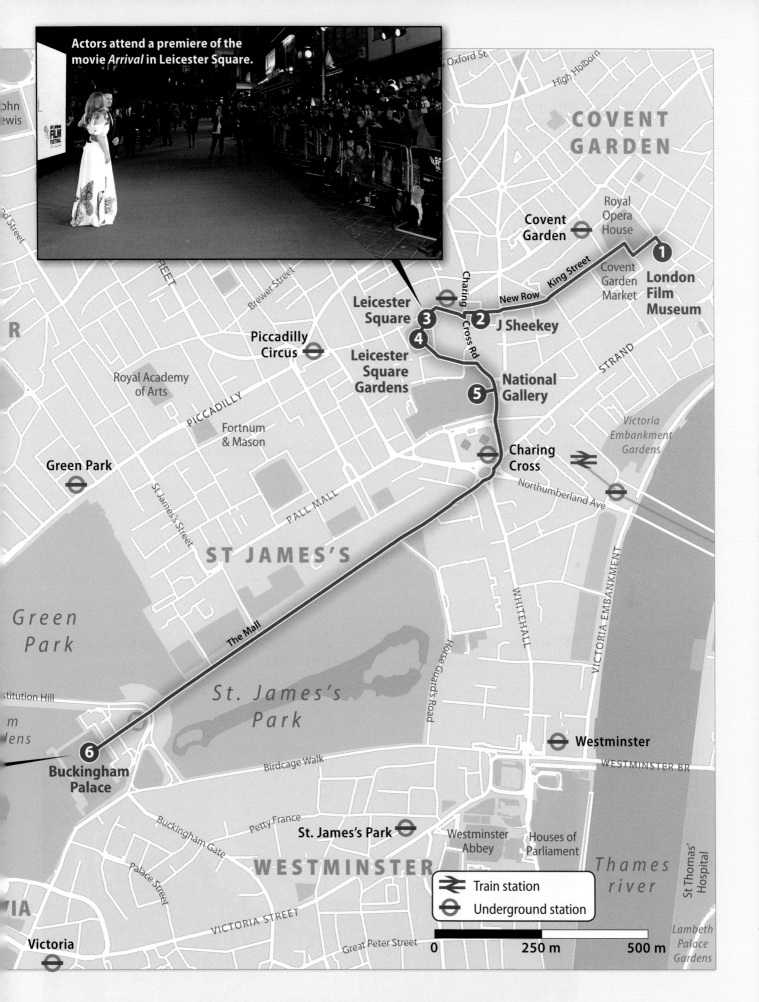

Actors attend a premiere of the movie *Arrival* in Leicester Square.

COVENT GARDEN

Royal Opera House

Covent Garden

King Street

Covent Garden Market

1

London Film Museum

New Row

Charing Cross Rd

2 J Sheekey

STRAND

Leicester Square **3**

4

Piccadilly Circus

Leicester Square Gardens

5 National Gallery

Royal Academy of Arts

Victoria Embankment Gardens

Brewer Street

PICCADILLY

Fortnum & Mason

Green Park

PALL MALL

Charing Cross

Northumberland Ave

St James's Street

ST JAMES'S

VICTORIA EMBANKMENT

Green Park

The Mall

St. James's Park

WHITEHALL

Horse Guard's Road

stitution Hill

m dens

6

Buckingham Palace

Birdcage Walk

Westminster

WESTMINSTER BR

Buckingham Gate

Petty France

St. James's Park

Westminster Abbey

Houses of Parliament

Thames river

Palace Street

WESTMINSTER

St Thomas' Hospital

VICTORIA STREET

Great Peter Street

Victoria

VIA

Train station
Underground station

0   250 m   500 m

Lambeth Palace Gardens

UNDERSTANDING THE READING

UNDERSTANDING
PURPOSE

A What kind of person would find the reading passage most useful? Circle the best option.

    a. someone who wants to know the best places to watch movies in London

    b. a visitor to London who is interested in movies and movie stars

    c. a first-time tourist who wants to see the most famous places in London

UNDERSTANDING
DETAILS

B Where can you do the following? Match each one with a location (1–6) as labeled on the map.

    1. _____ see a statue of a famous person who wrote plays

    2. _____ see people performing on the street

    3. _____ have some good food for a good price

    4. _____ see some famous paintings

    5. _____ see objects that appeared in movies

UNDERSTANDING
DETAILS

C Match each location with the movie in which it appeared. One location is used twice.

    1. *Skyfall* _____

    2. *The BFG* _____

    3. *Thor: The Dark World* _____

    4. *The King's Speech* _____

    5. *Harry Potter and the Half-Blood Prince* _____

    a. Charing Cross Underground Station

    b. Buckingham Palace

    c. the National Gallery

    d. Leicester Square Underground Station

CRITICAL THINKING:
APPLYING

D Which type of tour would be best for your town? Check (✓) one on the list or make up your own. Then discuss your ideas with a partner.

☐ a movie tour   ☐ a book tour   ☐ a music tour   ☐ a food tour

☐ a history tour   ☐ an art tour   ☐ _____

▶ **The Mall, leading to Buckingham Palace**

Writing

EXPLORING WRITTEN ENGLISH

A Read the sentences from the reading passages and answer the question below.

1. To get away from the crowds, you <u>should spend</u> some time in Leicester Square Gardens.

2. <u>Sleep</u> in your garden for a night.

3. And while you're there, you <u>should check out</u> some of the amazing street performers.

4. <u>Go</u> on a journey to an island.

5. <u>Choose</u> a river and travel to where it starts.

What do the underlined verbs do?

a. talk about something that happened in the past

b. give the reader reasons

c. tell the reader to do something

LANGUAGE FOR WRITING Using Imperatives and *Should*

You can use the imperative form of verbs when you are giving instructions. The imperative form looks like the base form of a verb. You don't need to put a subject in front of an imperative verb. The subject is understood to be "you."

> ***Climb*** *a hill that you can see from your town.*
> ***Take*** *a friend on their first microadventure.*
> ***Walk*** *down King Street to New Row.*

To make a negative imperative sentence, add *don't* before the verb.

> ***Don't take*** *the subway to the museum. It's quicker if you take a bus.*

You can use the modal verb *should* to give advice or instructions. Use the base form of the verb with *should*.

> *In San Francisco, you **should walk** across the Golden Gate Bridge.*
> *You **should take** a walking tour of Chicago.*

To make a negative statement, use *not* after *should*.
> *You **should not (shouldn't) go** on a bus tour. It's too expensive.*

◀ **San Francisco's Golden Gate Bridge**

B Unscramble the words and phrases to make sentences.

1. right / the street / turn / at the end of / .

   _____

2. at the Haymarket Theatre / should / you / see a play / .

   _____

3. should / you / at a local restaurant / lunch / have / .

   _____

4. the Louvre Museum / the Mona Lisa / at / go / to / see / .

   _____

5. go / afternoon / on / don't / the museum / a Saturday / to / .

   _____

6. you / Rome walking tour / start / at / should / the Trevi Fountain / your / .

   _____

C Complete each sentence (1–7) with the affirmative or negative form of the imperative or *should*.

1. (*try to learn*) _____ the local language before you move to another country.

2. (*travel*) _____ alone in dangerous places.

3. (*carry*) _____ a lot of cash when you're in a busy place.

4. (*study*) _____ hard before you take an exam.

5. (*use*) _____ your cell phone while driving.

6. (*feed*) _____ the animals when you visit a zoo.

7. (*visit*) _____ the Taj Mahal if you go to India.

▶ **The Trevi Fountain, Rome**

D Complete the chart with notes about what a visitor to your town or city should and should not do.

Things You Should Do	Things You Shouldn't Do

Now use your notes to write sentences. Use *should / shouldn't* or an imperative phrase. *Example: If you visit London, you should use the bus to get around.*

1. _____
2. _____
3. _____
4. _____
5. _____
6. _____

E Write some directions from your school / university to a place nearby. Use imperatives. Look at the phrases in the box to help you.

> **Giving Directions**
> *turn left / right (onto George Road)*   *go straight*   *cross (the street)*
> *go past (the supermarket)*   *walk down / along (George Road)*

How to get to _____.

1. Go out of this building and turn _____.
2. _____
3. _____
4. _____
5. _____

WRITING TASK

GOAL You are going to write sentences on the following topic:
Write a walking tour of an area you know well.

PLANNING **A** Follow the steps to plan your writing.

- Think of an area you know well. Make a note of at least three places people should see on a walking tour.
- Make notes on any interesting information about each place—the history, what you can do or see, and other facts.
- Draw a map of the area you chose. Draw a line to show the route of your walking tour. Write numbers on the map to show the places people should visit.

FIRST DRAFT **B** Use your notes to write sentences to describe your walking tour. Use imperatives and *should*.

Start at _____

Information about place A: _____

_____

Introduce place B: *Next,* _____

Information about place B: _____

_____

Introduce place C: *Then* _____

Information about place C: _____

_____

EDITING **C** Now edit your draft. Correct mistakes with imperatives and *should*. Use the checklist on page 120.

UNIT REVIEW
Answer the following questions.

1. What is a microadventure?

_____

_____

2. What are some phrases you can use to give directions?

_____

_____

3. Do you remember the meanings of these words? Check (✔) the ones you know. Look back at the unit and review the ones you don't know.

Reading 1:

☐ across   ☐ adventure   ☐ anywhere

☐ choose   ☐ climb   ☐ hiking

☐ important   ☐ low-cost   ☐ map

☐ trip

Reading 2:

☐ amazing   ☐ capital   ☐ check out

☐ crowd   ☐ location AWL   ☐ museum

☐ nearby   ☐ tour

NOTES

Verbs: Present Progressive Tense

Scientists are measuring a giant sequoia tree in Sequoia National Park, California.

OBJECTIVES **Grammar:** To learn about present progressive tense
Vocabulary and Spelling: To study common words with the sound of <u>oy</u> as in b<u>oy</u>
Writing: To write about people who are doing different things right now

Can you write about what people are doing right now?

Grammar for Writing

It **is raining** now.   The sun **is not shining** now.   The man **is running** now.

Present Progressive Tense

✓ In **present progressive tense**, you use **am, is, are** with **verb + ing**.

> I **am eating**.

✓ You use present progressive tense to talk about an action that is happening now. Four common time phrases for present progressive tense are **now, right now, today,** and **this** _____.

> We **are watching** TV <u>now</u>.
>
> Michael usually drives to school, but <u>**right now**</u> he **is walking** to class.
>
> I **am working** hard <u>today</u>.
>
> It rained a lot last night, but the sun **is shining** <u>this</u> morning.

✓ To make a negative with present progressive, use **not** after **am/is/are**.

> we **are planning** → we **are** <u>not</u> **planning**

✓ Contractions are common in speaking, but they are not so common in formal or academic writing.

> <u>**we're**</u> **planning**   **we** <u>**aren't**</u> **planning**

✓ Verbs that do not show action are not common in present progressive tense. With non-action verbs, use simple present tense.

> Some students **need** help with their homework now. (This is correct)
>
> Some students <u>**are needing**</u> help with their homework now. (This is NOT correct.)

Present Progressive Tense

	work	eat	take	plan
Singular	I **am** work**ing**	I **am** eat**ing**	I **am** tak**ing**	I **am** plan**ning**
	you **are** work**ing**	you **are** eat**ing**	you **are** tak**ing**	you **are** plan**ning**
	he **is** work**ing**	he **is** eat**ing**	he **is** tak**ing**	he **is** plan**ning**
	she **is** work**ing**	she **is** eat**ing**	she **is** tak**ing**	she **is** plan**ning**
	it **is** work**ing**	it **is** eat**ing**	it **is** tak**ing**	it **is** plan**ning**
Plural	we **are** work**ing**	we **are** eat**ing**	we **are** tak**ing**	we **are** plan**ning**
	you **are** work**ing**	you **are** eat**ing**	you **are** tak**ing**	you **are** plan**ning**
	they **are** work**ing**	they **are** eat**ing**	they **are** tak**ing**	they **are** plan**ning**

✓ In present progressive tense, add **–ing** to an action verb.

work → work**ing**   eat → eat**ing**

✓ For verbs that end in **–e**, drop the **–e** and add **–ing**.

take → tak**ing**

✓ For verbs that end in **–ie**, change **–ie** to **–y** and add **–ing**.

lie → l**ying**

Single or Double Consonant?

One Syllable	
+ –ing	double consonant + –ing
clean**ing**	pla**nn**ing
wash**ing**	sto**pp**ing

Two Syllables	
+ –ing	double consonant + –ing
open**ing**	occu**rr**ing
happen**ing**	permi**tt**ing

✓ For one-syllable verbs that end in consonant + vowel + consonant (CVC), double the last letter before adding **–ing.**

plan → pla**nn**ing

✓ For two-syllable verbs that end in consonant + vowel + consonant (CVC), double the last letter before adding **–ing** if the pronunciation stress is on the second syllable.

1̄ 2   1 2̄

o pen → open**ing**   be **gin** → begi**nn**ing

ACTIVITY 1 Identifying Verbs in Present Progressive Tense

Read this information about a man on an airplane. Underline the eight examples of present progressive tense. Then write them on the correct lines.

Jacob is a passenger on Flight 873. He is flying to California. He is going there because his company is doing business there. Right now Jacob is not talking to anyone. He is not eating anything. He is not drinking anything. Jacob is working on his computer. He is listening to his favorite music. He is a very happy person right now.

subject + am / is / are (not) + verb + ing

1. _____ _____ _____

2. _____ _____ _____

3. _____ _____ _____

4. _____ _____ _____

subject + am / is / are (not) + verb + ing

5. _____ _____ _____

6. _____ _____ _____

7. _____ _____ _____

8. _____ _____ _____

Practicing –ing Forms of 30 Common Verbs in Writing*

Write the –**ing** form of the 30 most common verbs in English writing.

verb	–ing form	verb	–ing form
1. go	_____	**16.** watch	_____
2. try	_____	**17.** give	_____
3. look	_____	**18.** sit	_____
4. make	_____	**19.** wait	_____
5. get	_____	**20.** live	_____
6. use	_____	**21.** see	_____
7. say	_____	**22.** leave	_____
8. come	_____	**23.** stand	_____
9. work	_____	**24.** hold	_____
10. talk	_____	**25.** tell	_____
11. take	_____	**26.** ask	_____
12. run	_____	**27.** think	_____
13. play	_____	**28.** move	_____
14. decide	_____	**29.** put	_____
15. try	_____	**30.** follow	_____

Source: Corpus of Contemporary American English

ACTIVITY 3 Writing Sentences with Present Progressive Tense

Use one word from each of the three groups to make five new sentences. Be careful with capital letters, verb form (–**ing**), and periods.

Subject	Action	Time
she	live in Canada	now
I	try to find a new job	right now
they	sit on a bench	at this moment

1. _____

2. _____

3. _____

4. _____

5. _____

ACTIVITY 4 PAIR WORK: Who Has the Most Sentences that Are Different?

Work with another student. Compare your sentences from Activity 3. You receive one point for each sentence that your partner does not have.

    1st time: _____ / 5 points possible

When you finish, work with another student. Each different sentence receives one point.

    2nd time: _____ / 5 points possible

    Your total: _____ / 10 points possible

Common Student Mistakes

Student Mistake X	Problem	Correct Example ✓
Jessica **is eating** lunch at 12:30 every day.	wrong tense	Jessica **eats** lunch at 12:30 every day.
Jessica **eats** lunch right now.	wrong tense	Jessica **is eating** lunch right now.
Now **we planning** our vacation.	form of **be** missing	Now we **are** planning our vacation.
Ali and I are **cook** spaghetti now.	–**ing** verb ending missing	Ali and I are cook**ing** spaghetti now.
I am **writeing** an e-mail now.	verb not spelled correctly	I am **writing** an e-mail now.
Some students **are needing** help with their homework now.	present progressive with non-action verb	Some students **need** help with their homework now.

26 **UNIT 2** • Verbs: Present Progressive Tense

ACTIVITY 5 **Correcting Mistakes with Present Progressive Verbs in Context**

Each sentence has a mistake with a verb. Correct this mistake and write the sentence again. Pay attention to capital letters and periods.

A Family Vacation

1. the johnson family taking a trip today

_____

2. they are go to california

_____

3. mr. johnson is driveing

_____

4. the children listen to the radio

_____

5. they are enjoy this trip very much

_____

Change the order of the words to write a correct sentence. Be careful with spelling, capital letters, punctuation, and word order.

At the Supermarket

1. at the supermarket now lucas is shopping right

   _____

2. many things he buying is

   _____

3. dinner for cousin's planning a lucas is his big birthday

   _____

4. delicious dinner for tonight's getting some big food he is

   _____

5. right waiting in now is lucas line

   _____

6. but the hard little cashier she is a is working very slow

   _____

7. lucas is watch his he is thinking about the because looking at time

   _____

8. great cousin to his a have lucas wants dinner with

   _____

Finding and Correcting 10 Mistakes

Circle the ten mistakes. Then write the sentences correctly. The number in parentheses ( ) is the number of mistakes in that sentence. Be ready to explain your answers.

A Day at the Zoo

1. Much people are visit the zoo today. (2)

   _____

2. Two giraffes eating leaf from the tall trees. (2)

   _____

3. An elephant is drink some water. (1)

   _____

4. Right now some children are laugh at the monkeys funny. (2)

   _____

5. One child pointing to the sky because an airplane is fly overhead. (2)

   _____

6. Everyone has a good time at the zoo today. (1)

   _____

You will hear six sentences three times. Listen carefully and write the six sentences. The number in parentheses ( ) is the number of words. Be careful with capital letters and end punctuation.

1. _____ (13)

2. _____ (10)

3. _____ (13)

4. _____ (9)

5. _____ (6)

6. _____ (9)

ACTIVITY 9 **Practicing Grammar and Vocabulary in Model Writing**

Read the sentences in the paragraph very carefully. Fill in the missing words from the word bank. Circle the 23 letters that need to be capital letters. Add periods and commas in the correct places. Then copy the paragraph on your own paper.

son	care	put	so	because
not	last	floor	on	difficult
has	dead	made	in	folded

Time to Clean the Hill Family's House

1 mr and mrs hill and their four children live in a very big house _____ maple street _____ chicago. 2 their house _____ five bedrooms two bathrooms a kitchen a dining room a huge living room and a garage. 3 they cleaned their house _____ saturday. 4 mr hill took _____ of the yard. 5 he picked up all the _____ leaves and he put them in trash bags. 6 mrs. hill washed all the dishes, and she _____ them in the cupboard. 7 sarah mopped the kitchen _____ and anna _____ all the beds. 8 their youngest daughter _____ towels. 9 their _____ cleaned one of the bathrooms. 10 he did _____ like this job. 11 it was _____ to clean this big house _____ everyone helped. 12 _____ everyone did their jobs so well the hill family's house was beautiful.

ACTIVITY 10 Guided Writing: Making Changes in Model Writing

Write the sentences from Activity 9 again, but your new sentences are about right now. Make the changes listed below and all other necessary changes.

<u>Sentence 3</u>. Change **last Saturday** to **today**. Then change the verb tense of all the action verbs.

<u>Sentences 9 and 10</u>. Combine these two sentences with a good connecting word. Use the simple present tense for the verb **like**.

<u>Sentence 12</u>. Write a new sentence that talks about their house all the time. In other words, the sentence should be a fact, not only a statement about right now.

_____

_____

_____

_____

_____

_____

_____

_____

_____

_____

_____

Building Vocabulary and Spelling

Learning Words with the Sound of oy as in boy*

oy = b **oy**   This sound is usually spelled with the letters **oy** and **oi.**

b o y

c o i n

ACTIVITY 11 **Which Words Do You Know?**

This list has 16 words with the sound of **oy** in b**oy**.

1. Notice the spelling patterns.

2. Check ✓ the words you know.

3. Look up new words in a dictionary. Write the meanings in your Vocabulary Notebook.

Common Words

GROUP 1:
Words spelled with **oy**

- ☐ 1. b o y
- ☐ 2. d e s t r o y
- ☐ 3. e m p l o y e e
- ☐ 4. e m p l o y e r
- ☐ 5. e n j o y
- ☐ 6. j o y
- ☐ 7. t o y

GROUP 2:
Words spelled with **oi**

- ☐ 8. b o i l
- ☐ 9. c h o i c e
- ☐ 10. c o i n
- ☐ 11. j o i n
- ☐ 12. n o i s e
- ☐ 13. o i l
- ☐ 14. p o i n t
- ☐ 15. p o i s o n
- ☐ 16. v o i c e

*List is from: Spelling Vocabulary List © 2013 Keith Folse

ACTIVITY 12 Matching Words and Pictures

Use the list in Activity 11 to write the common word that matches the picture.

1. _____

5. _____

2. _____

6. _____

3. _____

7. _____

4. _____

8. _____

ACTIVITY 13 Spelling Words with the Sound of oy in boy

Fill in the missing letters to spell words with the sound of **oy** in b**oy**. Then copy the correct word.

1. enj __   _____

2. p __ nt   _____

3. empl __ er   _____

4. destr __   _____

5. ch __ ce   _____

6. v __ ce   _____

7. b __ l   _____

8. c __ n   _____

ACTIVITY 14 Writing Sentences with Vocabulary in Context

Complete each sentence with the correct word from Activity 13. Then copy the sentence with correct capital letters, commas, and end punctuation.

1. an orange a tennis ball and a .... are examples of round things

   _____

2. who is your ....

   _____

3. a strong storm can .... houses and buildings

   _____

4. it takes about four or five minutes to .... an egg

   _____

5. the three arrows .... to the location of the cash machine

   _____

6. for the main course of your dinner you have a .... of chicken fish or beef

   _____

7. most people do not .... movies with sad endings

   _____

8. people want to listen to her songs because she has an incredible ....

   _____

ACTIVITY 15   Scrambled Letters

Change the order of the letters to write a word that has the sound of **oy** in b**oy**.

_____ **1.** c h c e o i

_____ **2.** e c o i v

_____ **3.** j y o

_____ **4.** l o i

_____ **5.** e e e o m p l y

_____ **6.** e s i o n

_____ **7.** b i o l

_____ **8.** n i o j

_____ **9.** y o b

_____ **10.** d e t r s o y

_____ **11.** j y o e n

_____ **12.** s o p i o n

_____ **13.** y o t

_____ **14.** t o i n p

Track 4))) **ACTIVITY 16   Spelling Practice**

Write the word that you hear. You will hear each word two times.

1. _____   **6.** _____   **11.** _____

2. _____   **7.** _____   **12.** _____

3. _____   **8.** _____   **13.** _____

4. _____   **9.** _____   **14.** _____

5. _____   **10.** _____   **15.** _____

ACTIVITY 17   Spelling Review: Which Word Is Correct?

This review covers the different ways of spelling **oy** in b**oy** in this unit. Read each pair of words. Circle the word that is spelled correctly.

	A	B		A	B
1.	boyl	boil	**9.**	choyce	choice
2.	boy	boi	**10.**	voyce	voice
3.	oyl	oil	**11.**	joy	joi
4.	destroy	destroi	**12.**	enjoy	enjoi
5.	poyson	poison	**13.**	coyn	coin
6.	poynt	point	**14.**	noyse	noise
7.	employee	emploiee	**15.**	employer	emploier
8.	joyn	join			

ACTIVITY 18 Spelling Review

Read the four words in each row. Underline the word that is spelled correctly.

	A	B	C	D
1.	shoice	choice	choise	echoise
2.	nex	naxt	next	nax
3.	gools	goals	gouls	goels
4.	suger	asugar	esugar	sugar
5.	bcause	bcose	becose	because
6.	reason	reeson	raison	rason
7.	with	weth	whit	whith
8.	piple	beeble	people	peepl
9.	tomorrow	tomorow	tamorrow	temorow
10.	famil	familia	famili	family
11.	dstroy	destroie	distroy	destroy
12.	spind	spnd	spend	espend
13.	enclude	include	includ	enclud
14.	shwer	eshower	showr	shower
15.	doctere	doctor	dokter	ductor
16.	righ	rait	right	raight
17.	noyse	niose	noise	nois
18.	allways	alwes	allwes	always
19.	doughter	duter	doter	daughter
20.	hungry	hungrey	hungri	humgrey

Original Student Writing

Writing Your Ideas in Sentences or a Paragraph

Write eight to twelve sentences on your own paper. Write about people who are doing different things right now. For example, write about some people in a restaurant, in school, in a park, or another place. Use the present progressive tense. For help, you can follow the examples in Activity 9 (page 30) and Activity 10 (page 31).

Peer Editing

Exchange papers from the above activity. Read your partner's sentences.
Then use Peer Editing Sheet 1 on ELTNGL.com/sites/els to make comments about the writing.

NOTES

THE VISUAL AGE

3

A group of people take selfies at the Amman Citadel, Jordan.

THINK AND DISCUSS

1 Do you take a lot of pictures? What do you take pictures of?
2 Do you share pictures online? Which ones?

A Look at the information on these pages and answer the questions.

1. What are some ways that photography has changed since it was invented?

2. Why has the number of photographs taken increased so much in recent years?

B Match the correct form of the words in blue to their definitions.

_____ (n) a picture made with a camera

_____ (v) to put on a website for other people to see

_____ (n) people who use computers, software, or websites

TAKING PICTURES

The graph on this page shows moments in the history of photography. Between 2011 and 2017, more **photos** were taken than in all history before 2011: more than five trillion (5,000,000,000,000).

This huge increase is mainly because of the rise of smartphones and social media. Facebook **users** share over 300 million photos every day, and Instagram users **post** more than 80 million photos a day. It seems that today we really are living in a visual age.

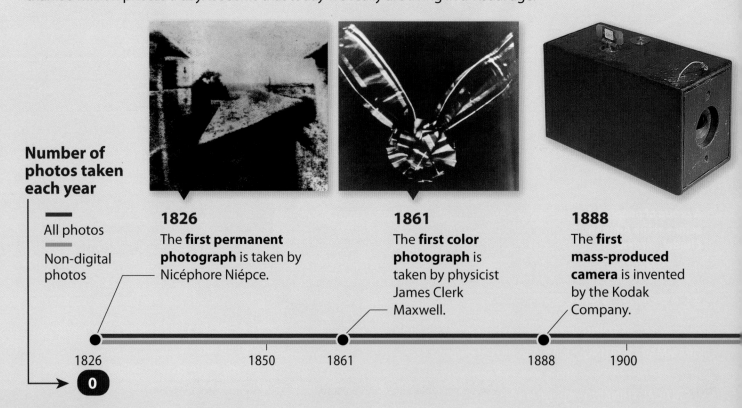

Number of photos taken each year

— All photos

— Non-digital photos

1826
The **first permanent photograph** is taken by Nicéphore Niépce.

1861
The **first color photograph** is taken by physicist James Clerk Maxwell.

1888
The **first mass-produced camera** is invented by the Kodak Company.

| 1826 | 1850 | 1861 | 1888 | 1900 |

0

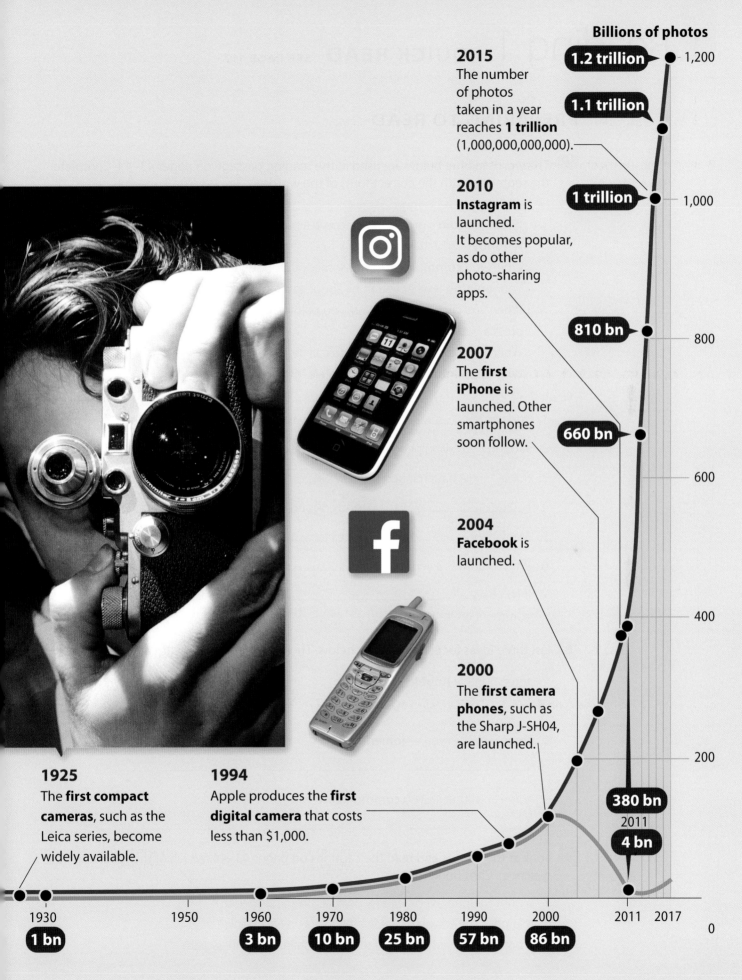

Billions of photos

2015
The number of photos taken in a year reaches **1 trillion** (1,000,000,000,000).

1.2 trillion — 1,200

1.1 trillion

2010
Instagram is launched. It becomes popular, as do other photo-sharing apps.

1 trillion — 1,000

2007
The **first iPhone** is launched. Other smartphones soon follow.

810 bn — 800

660 bn

2004
Facebook is launched.

— 600

— 400

2000
The **first camera phones**, such as the Sharp J-SH04, are launched.

— 200

380 bn
2011
4 bn

1925
The **first compact cameras**, such as the Leica series, become widely available.

1994
Apple produces the **first digital camera** that costs less than $1,000.

1930   1950   1960   1970   1980   1990   2000   2011   2017   0

1 bn   **3 bn**   **10 bn**   **25 bn**   **57 bn**   **86 bn**

Reading 1 QUICK READ SEE PAGE 112

PREPARING TO READ

BUILDING
VOCABULARY **A** The words in **blue** below are used in the reading passage on pages 43–44. Complete the sentences with the correct form of the words.

> When you **join** a group, you become a part of that group.
>
> A **hobby** is an activity you do for fun.
>
> When you **communicate** with someone, you share information.
>
> Your **opinion** is what you think about something.
>
> When you **click on** something, you point at it using your computer mouse and press a button.
>
> When you **contact** someone, you call them or write to them.
>
> When you **find out** something, you learn about it.

1. You can _____ how to do many things on the website wikiHow.

2. Around two billion people have _____ Facebook since it began.

3. Social media has changed the way we _____ with friends and family.

4. I _____ the wrong link and went to a strange website.

5. Many people use social media sites to _____ old friends.

6. Photography is a very popular _____ these days.

7. If you have a(n) _____ about an online article, you can post a comment on it.

USING
VOCABULARY **B** List three ideas for each category below. Then share your ideas with a partner.

1. three popular **hobbies**

   _____   _____   _____

2. three websites you've **joined**

   _____   _____   _____

3. three apps that let you **communicate** with your friends

   _____   _____   _____

PREVIEWING **C** Look at the photos and read the captions on pages 43–44. Which of the following best describes Chris Burkard?

a. a photographer who became popular on social media

b. a famous surfer who has many followers on Facebook

c. a businessman who created the photo-sharing app Instagram

Photos like this, of a surfer in California, have helped Chris Burkard gain a huge following on Instagram.

SHARING SUCCESS

🎧 Track 5

A From a young age, photography was more than just a hobby for Chris Burkard. His amazing photos of surfers in wild locations helped him start a successful career. In 2013, however, something happened that took his career to new heights.

B While on a photography trip in Iceland, a surfer introduced Burkard to a photo-sharing app called Instagram. Burkard decided to join, and started posting images. Four years later, he had over 2 million Instagram followers.

C Photo-sharing sites like Instagram, Imgur, and Flickr are getting more and more popular. In 2011, Instagram had 5 million users. By 2016, that number was 500 million. Sites like these are helping photographers like Burkard connect with a large number of people.

So how do you make a successful photo-sharing account? Here are some tips that might help you become the next Chris Burkard.

1. **Be yourself. Be different.** Don't try to be like anyone else. Create your own unique style.

2. **Get connected.** Share posts from your photo-sharing account on other social media sites. When people see your posts, they might click on them and go to your photo-sharing account.

3. **Choose hashtags carefully.** Look at other accounts to find out which hashtags are popular, and use them. For example, many people use the hashtag #getoutside for photos of the outdoors. There are about 6 million Instagram photos with that hashtag. So if you use it, people who like these 6 million photos will be more likely to find you.

4. Contact **other people.** Follow and comment on other users' posts. When you do this, they are more likely to post comments on yours.

5. Communicate **with your followers.** Make them feel like they are part of a community.[1] For example, ask questions in your captions, and share your own ideas and opinions.

[1] A **community** is a group of people who live in the same area or who have similar interests.

Burkard took this photo in the Aleutian Islands, Alaska.

UNDERSTANDING THE READING

A Complete the summary with information from the reading passage.

In ¹_____, Chris Burkard was introduced to the photo-sharing app Instagram.
Burkard already had a successful career in ²_____. He was well-known for his
amazing photos of ³_____. But the photo-sharing app helped take his career
to a new level. By ⁴_____, Burkard had more than 2 million followers. Other
photographers are also finding that image-sharing sites like Instagram, ⁵_____,
and ⁶_____ are helping them connect with a huge audience.

B Check (✓) the advice that the author of the article would agree with.

☐ a. Use hashtags that nobody else is using.
☐ b. Share your opinions when you post a photo.
☐ c. It's a good idea to comment on other people's posts.
☐ d. Try to post photos that are different from other people's.
☐ e. Use only one social media site to post your photos.

C Find and underline the following words in the reading on pages 43–44. Use the
context to help you understand the meaning. Then write each word next to its
definition.

wild (paragraph A)	**followers** (paragraph B)	**unique** (paragraph D)

1. _____ (adj) different from everything else
2. _____ (adj) natural, not controlled by people
3. _____ (n) people who receive news and updates about someone
   else on social media

> **CRITICAL THINKING**   **Applying** means using an idea in a new way. For
> example, if you read an article that gives advice, try to apply that advice to your own
> situation. This can help you understand the advice better.

D Imagine you are setting up a new Instagram account and want to be successful. Use
your own ideas and the advice given in the article to answer the questions.

1. What would you take photos of?

   _____

2. What website or app would you use to share your photos?

   _____

3. What would make your photos unique?

   _____

4. What hashtags would you use?

   _____

DEVELOPING READING SKILLS

> **READING SKILL** Identifying Examples
>
> Writers use certain words and phrases to introduce examples.
>
> *Social media sites **like** Facebook and Twitter have become popular in many countries.*
>
> *There are several things you can do to take better selfies. **For example**, make sure you are facing the light.*
>
> Remember to use a comma after *For example*.

IDENTIFYING
EXAMPLES

A These sentences are from the reading passage on pages 43–44. Underline the examples.

1. Photo-sharing sites like Instagram, Imgur, and Flickr are getting more and more popular.

2. Choose hashtags carefully. Look at other accounts to find out which hashtags are popular, and use them. For example, many people use the hashtag #getoutside for photos of the outdoors.

3. Communicate with your followers. Make them feel like they are part of a community. For example, ask questions in your captions, and share your own ideas and opinions.

IDENTIFYING
EXAMPLES

B Match the examples (a–e) to the sentences or sentence parts (1–5).

1. There are many search engines you can use, ___

2. You can share many different types of things on social media sites. ___

3. Some of the most popular images on Instagram are of cute animals ___

4. Edit your photos before you post them. ___

5. Hashtags ___

a. For example, you can post photos, videos, text, and links to other websites.

b. like #love, #cute, and #selfie are very popular.

c. like Google and Bing.

d. For example, use photo editing apps that make your pictures look clearer or brighter.

e. like cats or dogs.

IDENTIFYING
EXAMPLES

C Go back to Reading 2 in Unit 1 on page 12. Look at the paragraphs listed below and find:

1. an example of a play written by William Shakespeare (paragraph E)

   _____

2. two examples of artists whose work is in the National Gallery, London (paragraph F)

   _____

3. two examples of movies in which Buckingham Palace appears (paragraph G)

   _____

Video

Franz Lanting's photo of African elephants in Botswana has been "liked" over a million times on Instagram.

A MILLION "LIKES"

BEFORE VIEWING

A Look at the photo and read the caption. Why do you think this image was so popular?

DISCUSSION

B Read the information about Instagram. Then answer the questions.

LEARNING ABOUT
THE TOPIC

Since its launch in 2010, Instagram has become one of the most widely used image-sharing apps in the world. Around 90 percent of Instagram users are under the age of 35. Many of the most popular accounts are held by famous people. Taylor Swift, for example, has over 100 million Instagram followers. Photos of the natural world are also popular. One of the most popular accounts belongs to National Geographic. The photos posted by the organization have been "liked" more than 3 billion times.

1. What kinds of Instagram accounts have the most followers?

   _____

2. What kinds of photos do you think National Geographic posts on Instagram?

   _____

C The words in **bold** below are used in the video. Match the correct form of each word with its definition.

> The Asian elephant is an **endangered species**. Not many remain in the wild.
> It's possible to take some great photos at **dawn**.
> A female tiger usually gives birth to three or four **cubs**.

1. _____ (n) the time of day when the sun is coming up

2. _____ (n) a young wild animal, such as a bear or lion

3. _____ (n) a group of animals that could disappear

WHILE VIEWING

UNDERSTANDING
MAIN IDEAS

A ▶ Watch the video. Check (✓) the three things that are true about all the photos in the video.

☐ They are all photos of animals.
☐ They all received over a million "likes" on Instagram.
☐ They were all taken by the same photographer.
☐ They were all posted on National Geographic's Instagram account.

UNDERSTANDING
DETAILS

B ▶ Watch the video again. Match the sentence parts to describe the photos.

1. The photo of the elephants ____
2. The photo of the birds ____
3. The photo of the leopard ____
4. The photo of the whale ____
5. The photo of the tigers ____

a. was taken in the evening.
b. made the photographer cry.
c. was taken in the early morning.
d. is part of a project to save endangered species.
e. shows just a part of the animal.

AFTER VIEWING

REACTING TO
THE VIDEO

A Which photo do you like the best? Why? Discuss with a partner.

REACTING TO
THE VIDEO

B Which photo in the video do you think was most difficult to capture? Why? Note your ideas below and then discuss with a partner.

_____

_____

Reading 2 QUICK READ SEE PAGE 115

PREPARING TO READ

A The words in **blue** below are used in the reading passage on pages 50–51. Complete the sentences with the correct form of the words.

BUILDING VOCABULARY

> **direction** (n) the general line that something moves along
>
> **prize** (n) something you receive if you win a competition
>
> **shadow** (n) a dark shape made when you block light
>
> **appear** (v) to become possible to be seen
>
> **believe** (v) to think something is true
>
> **guess** (v) to give an answer or opinion without being sure it is correct
>
> **missing** (adj) not able to be seen or found
>
> **real** (adj) not false or fake

1. Can you _____ which of these two photos is not _____?

2. When taking a photo, it's important to consider the _____ the light is coming from.

3. Your _____ gets longer in the evening when the sun is low in the sky.

4. The police officer showed me a photo of a _____ person he was looking for.

5. The photographer waited for a long time before a shark _____ from below the water.

6. He told me the photo was real, but I didn't _____ him.

7. My friend won a $100 _____ in a photography competition.

B Note answers to the questions below. Then share your ideas with a partner.

USING VOCABULARY

1. Can you remember a photo or piece of news that **appeared** on social media but was not **real**? What was it?

   _____

2. Did you **believe** the story / photo at first, or could you **guess** that it was fake?

   _____

C Read the first paragraph of the reading on pages 50–51. Discuss the question with a partner. Check your ideas as you read the passage.

PREVIEWING

IS IT REAL?

A   Look at the two shark photos on page 51. One is **real**, but the other is fake.[1] Can you tell which is which?

B   In 2016, a dramatic[2] photo of a great white shark jumping out of the water **appeared** on Twitter and went viral.[3] The person who posted the photo called himself Bob Burton. He said he was National Geographic's top photographer, and that the picture was National Geographic's photo of the year.

C   But none of this was true. There is no one called Bob Burton at National Geographic. There isn't even a National Geographic **prize** for photo of the year. And, most importantly, the photo itself wasn't real—it was made on a computer by joining together several[4] other photos.

D   With computer technology and social media, it is much easier now to make and share fake images. So how is it possible to tell if a photo is real? First, look for a source. Where does the photo come from? Is there a photographer's name? Can you find any information about them on the Internet? Second, look for clues in the photo. Sometimes the **direction** of light and **shadows** is wrong. Is anything in the photo too big or too small, or is anything **missing**?

E   So did you **guess** correctly? The fake photo is the one at the top of the page. When you look closely, you can see that something is not quite right. The movement and shape of the water don't look natural. The lighting also looks a little too bright. The one below it, however, is completely real. This amazing photo was taken by Chris Fallows. Fallows has spent much of his career photographing sharks. For this photo, he waited in his boat for a whole day to get the image he wanted.

F   New technology is changing how we create and share images. But don't **believe** everything you see!

[1] If something is **fake**, it is not real.
[2] If something is **dramatic**, it is exciting and amazing.
[3] If something **goes viral**, it spreads around the Internet very quickly.
[4] **Several** refers to a small number that is more than two.

UNDERSTANDING THE READING

UNDERSTANDING
THE GIST

A Which of the following would be the best alternative title for the passage?

a. National Geographic's Best Shark Photos
b. Don't Believe Everything You See
c. Famous Photos that Went Viral

UNDERSTANDING
DETAILS

B Read the sentences. Circle **T** for true or **F** for false.

1. Photo A on page 51 was popular on the Internet.   **T**   **F**

2. Bob Burton is the name of a National Geographic photographer.   **T**   **F**

3. Every year, National Geographic gives a prize for photo of the year.   **T**   **F**

4. Photo A on page 51 was made using a computer.   **T**   **F**

5. Chris Fallows has spent a lot of time photographing sharks.   **T**   **F**

UNDERSTANDING
DETAILS

C What are two clues that can help you decide if a photo is real or fake? Note your
answers below. Then discuss with a partner.

1. _____

   For example, _____

2. _____

   For example, _____

CRITICAL THINKING:
APPLYING

D How can you decide if a news story you see on social media is real or fake? Use the
ideas in the passage to help. Note your ideas below. Then discuss with a partner.

_____

_____

_____

_____

CRITICAL THINKING:
EVALUATING

E Note answers to the questions below. Then share your ideas with a partner.

1. Why do you think people create fake photos or fake news stories?

   _____

   _____

2. What problems can fake information cause?

   _____

   _____

Writing

EXPLORING WRITTEN ENGLISH

A Read the sentences below and answer the question.

NOTICING

1. He waited in his boat for a whole day <u>to get the image he wanted</u>.

2. Someone put several photos together <u>to create the picture</u>.

3. In the past, people sent their camera film to a shop <u>to get photos printed</u>.

4. Look at other accounts <u>to find out which hashtags are popular</u>, and use them.

What do the underlined words describe?

a. places   b. reasons   c. times

LANGUAGE FOR WRITING Infinitives of Purpose

An infinitive is the base form of a verb starting with *to* (e.g., *to send, to share, to communicate, to find out*). We can use an infinitive of purpose when we want to say *why* or *for what reason* someone does something.

Why do you spend time on social media?

*I spend time on social media **to see** what my friends are doing and **to find out** what is happening in the world.*

Why do you post photos of food?

*I post photos of food **to show** people what I'm eating.*

You can also start a sentence with an infinitive of purpose. A comma is needed to separate the clauses.

***To chat** with my friends, I use WhatsApp.*

B Match the sentence parts to make full sentences.

1. I use my dictionary app ____   a. to take photos.

2. Many people use Instagram ____   b. to share photos with friends.

3. Most people use their smartphones ____   c. to look up new words.

C Rewrite each sentence in **B** with the infinitive phrase at the start of the sentence.

1. To take photos, _____

2. To share _____

3. _____

D Write answers to the questions using infinitives of purpose. Use your own ideas.

1. Why do most people use social media sites like Facebook?

   _____

2. What app do you use the most? Why do you use it?

   _____

3. Why do you think many people still use email?

   _____

NOTICING **E** Read the sentences and answer the question below.

1. He never thought he would be successful, <u>but</u> he was wrong.
2. Photo-sharing sites like Instagram <u>and</u> Flickr are getting more popular.
3. Is anything in the photo too big <u>or</u> too small?

What is the purpose of the underlined words?

a. to join ideas   b. to show cause and effect   c. to show the reason for something

---

LANGUAGE FOR WRITING Using *and*, *but*, and *or*

You can connect ideas in a sentence using *and*, *but*, and *or*.
Use *and* to connect two or more items. You can also use *and* to connect two sentences.
Use commas to separate three or more items in a series.
Use a comma to separate two sentences.

> *I use Facebook **and** Twitter to share information.*
> *I use Facebook, Twitter, Instagram, **and** Snapchat to share photos.*
> *I post on Instagram once a day, **and** I post on Imgur once a week.*

Or is used to show two or more choices. Use *or* to connect two or more items in a series or to connect two sentences.

> *Do you prefer to post photos on Facebook **or** Instagram?*
> *Right after I wake up, I usually log on to Facebook, Twitter, **or** Instagram.*
> *I can email the photo to you, **or** I can post it on Instagram.*

But shows two opposite or different ideas. Use *but* to connect two sentences.
Use a comma to separate the two sentences.

> *I like Facebook, **but** I don't like Twitter.*
> *I never post on Facebook, **but** I post a lot on Instagram.*

F Circle the correct conjunction in each sentence.

1. My tablet is useful, **but** / **or** it's quite heavy.

2. I log on to Facebook every day, **and** / **but** I don't often use Twitter.

3. I post photographs on Pinterest **or** / **but** Imgur, **and** / **but** I don't use Instagram.

4. When I wake up, I use my laptop **and** / **or** my tablet—whichever is closer to my bed.

5. I love my car's GPS, **but** / **and** sometimes it gives me the wrong directions.

6. When I ride the bus, I look at Facebook, send emails, **but** / **or** read on my tablet.

7. It's hard to park in the city, so I use an app to find a parking space **but** / **or** I take the subway.

8. I use my dictionary app **but** / **or** go to dictionary.com to look up new words.

G Write a conjunction to complete each sentence. Add commas where they are needed.

1. I post photos _____ videos every day.

2. I bought a new activity tracker to help me get healthier _____ I still don't exercise.

3. In the morning, I always have a cup of tea _____ coffee.

4. Send me an email _____ a text when you get off work.

5. We can order pizza online _____ we'll have to wait a long time before it arrives.

H Combine the sentences using conjunctions. Add commas where they are needed.

1. I use my laptop for work. I use my phone for social media.

   _____

2. Do you prefer Gmail? Do you prefer Yahoo?

   _____

3. Before I buy new technology, I read reviews. I get recommendations from my friends.

   _____

4. I use my phone to listen to podcasts. I use my phone to watch movies. I use my phone to send emails.

   _____

   _____

5. I can use my smartwatch to make phone calls. I prefer to call people on my smartphone.

   _____

6. I comment on people's photos on Facebook. I don't comment on news articles.

   _____

WRITING TASK

GOAL You are going to write sentences on the following topic:

Which websites or apps do you use a lot? What do you use them for?

PLANNING **A** Follow the steps to plan your sentences.

- Brainstorm five apps or websites that you use or visit often. Write them in the chart.
- Make notes about why you use each app or website. Think of two reasons for each.

Website / Name of App	Why?
1.	
2.	
3.	
4.	
5.	

FIRST DRAFT **B** Use your notes to write five sentences about the apps and websites that you use. Use infinitives of purpose and *and*, *but*, and *or*.

Example: I use WhatsApp to talk to my hockey team and to share pictures of our games.

EDITING **C** Now edit your draft. Correct mistakes with infinitives of purpose and using *and*, *but*, and *or*. Use the checklist on page 120.

UNIT REVIEW

Answer the following questions.

1. What are two ways to tell if a photo is fake?

_____

_____

2. What are three words that can be used to join ideas in a sentence?

_____

_____

3. Do you remember the meanings of these words? Check (✓) the ones you know. Look back at the unit and review the ones you don't know.

Reading 1:

☐ click on	☐ communicate AWL	☐ contact AWL
☐ find out	☐ hobby	☐ join
☐ opinion	☐ photo	☐ post
☐ user		

Reading 2:

☐ appear	☐ believe	☐ direction
☐ guess	☐ missing	☐ prize
☐ real	☐ shadow	

NOTES

People are enjoying
the night in Tokyo, Japan.

OBJECTIVES To learn the present progressive tense
To practice compound sentences with *and* and *so*
To learn complex sentences with the present
To practice adverbs of manner
To study prepositional phrases of place

Can you write about what is happening at this moment?

The Present Progressive Tense

We use the **present progressive tense** to describe actions that are happening in the current moment or an extended period of time in the present (for example: today, this week, this semester, this year).

Subject	Be	(*Not*)	Verb + -*ing*
I	am		eat**ing**
he / she / it	is	(not)	study**ing**
we / you / you (plural) / they	are		tak**ing**
			runn**ing**
			do**ing**

Stative (Non-action) Verbs

Be careful! Some verbs in English do <u>not</u> usually take the progressive tense because they are not action verbs. Here are some common **non-action**, or **stative**, verbs: *be, have, see, love, believe, own,* and *want.*

✗ I <u>am having</u> a new boss.

✓ I have a new boss.

✗ Mark <u>is not wanting</u> the gift.

✓ Mark does not want the gift.

ACTIVITY 1 Identifying the Present Progressive Tense

Underline the 17 present progressive verbs in the paragraph.

Example Paragraph 1

A Busy Tourist Site

In pictures, Machu Picchu, Peru, seems very **remote** and quiet, but it is often a very busy place! Right now, hundreds of tourists are arriving by bus and getting in line to enter the **site**. **Guards** are giving directions, and **hikers** from the Inca **Trail** are putting their heavy bags in lockers. Inside Machu Picchu, people are walking everywhere. They are looking at

remote: far away, distant

a site: a location, specific place

a guard: a person who protects another person or place

a hiker: a person who takes long walks for enjoyment

a trail: a path

the amazing **ruins** and taking lots of pictures. Guides are talking to travel groups about the history of this ancient site. Smaller groups of people are exploring the ruins by themselves. They are touching the stones and talking about the beauty all around them. One man is even touching the Sacred Rock in the northern square. Many visitors are standing in line and waiting to take a picture of themselves with the ruins in the background. Some people are walking up and down the **steep**, narrow steps and staircases very carefully. They are taking their time because the stones are wet. They do not want to fall down the slippery steps. Some adventurous tourists are walking up a mountain trail behind Machu Picchu so that they can see more of this amazing site. It is hard to believe that such an old and distant place can be so lively!

the ruins: the remains of something that is old and/or damaged

steep: going up/down at a high angle

Study the picture of Bruce and his friends. Then read the paragraph. Fill in the missing verbs based on the picture.

Example Paragraph 2

A University Student's Room

Tomorrow is a big day for Bruce. His mother is coming to visit him at college for the first time. Bruce is very excited, but he is also worried. His dorm room is a mess. This is why he called all his friends to come help him. His good friend Lina **1** _____ the floor because the carpet is very dirty. Bruce's friend Joe **2** _____ some of Bruce's clothes to the laundry. At the same time, Bruce's roommate Paul **3** _____ all of the empty pizza boxes and soda cans. Bruce **4** _____ . Bruce feels very lucky to have such good friends, and he is sure that the room will be ready for his mother's visit.

Describing a Scene

Write sentences that describe the action in the picture. Use the present progressive. Make at least one of your sentences negative.

1. _____

2. _____

3. _____

4. _____

5. _____

6. _____

7. _____

8. _____

Writer's Note

Avoiding Repetition in Compound Sentences

When you have the same noun in both parts of a compound sentence, you should use a pronoun after the connector. This helps avoid repetition.

Repetitive Writing (Using Only Nouns)	Better Writing (Using Nouns and Pronouns)
Jake is washing the car, so **Jake** is getting wet.	**Jake** is washing the car, so **he** is getting wet.
Tia is making **a lemon cake**, and **the lemon cake** smells good.	Tia is making **a lemon cake**, and **it** smells good.

Reviewing *And* and *So* in Compound Sentences

We use *and* in a compound sentence to show added information. We use *so* in a compound sentence to show cause and effect. The sentence after *so* shows the result (what happens because) of the first sentence.

ACTIVITY 4 **Practicing Compound Sentences with *And***

Match the sentences. Then combine the two sentences into a compound sentence using *and*.

Column A	Column B
~~Ann is watching television.~~	Oranges contain a lot of vitamin C.
Oranges taste great.	I hope the marigold seeds grow quickly.
Ecuador exports millions of cut flowers around the world.	~~Ann is texting her friends.~~
That blouse is the perfect color for you.	Alaska contains large amounts of oil.
I am planting marigold seeds.	Valia is making roast beef for her guests.
Alaska is a part of the United States.	That blouse matches your pants and handbag.
Valia is having guests for dinner tonight.	Colombia exports millions of cut flowers around the world, too.

1.   Ann is watching television, and she is texting her friends.

2.   _____

3.   _____

4.   _____

5.   _____

6.   _____

7.   _____

ACTIVITY 5 Combining Sentences with *So*

In each item, identify each sentence as a cause (*C*) or a result (*R*). Then combine them into a compound sentence using *so*. Put the cause first, then the connector *so*, and then the result. Use correct punctuation.

1a. ____*C*____ I am thirsty.

b. ____*R*____ I am drinking a huge glass of water.

_____I am thirsty, so I am drinking a huge glass of water._____

2a. _____ We are not playing tennis.

b. _____ It is raining really hard.

_____

3a. _____ Mr. Lopez is taking Ana to the doctor.

b. _____ Ana is very sick.

_____

4a. _____ The audience loves the show.

b. _____ The audience is applauding wildly.

_____

5a. _____ Jonathan is not feeling well.

b. _____ Jonathan is not going to the party.

_____

6a. _____ I am not buying the latest smart phone.

b. _____ The latest smart phone is very expensive.

_____

7a. _____ Brian is sleeping late today.

b. _____ Brian is extremely tired.

_____

8a. _____ Angela needs to buy some fruits and vegetables.

b. _____ Angela is shopping at the farmer's market.

_____

ACTIVITY 6 Scenarios: Writing Compound Sentences with *So* and the Present Progressive

Write a compound sentence with *so* to describe the action happening in the picture. Use the present progressive tense.

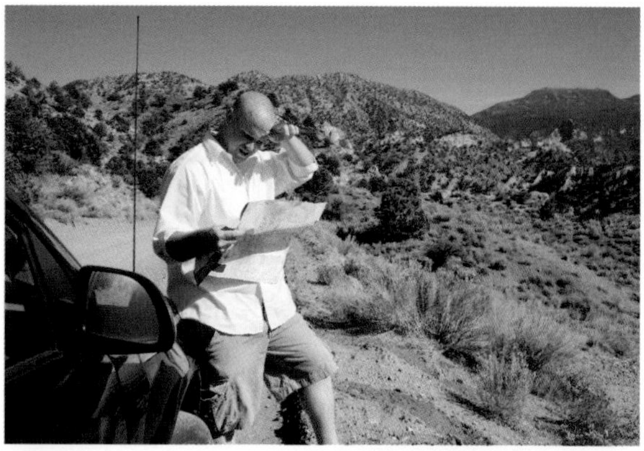

1. ______________________________

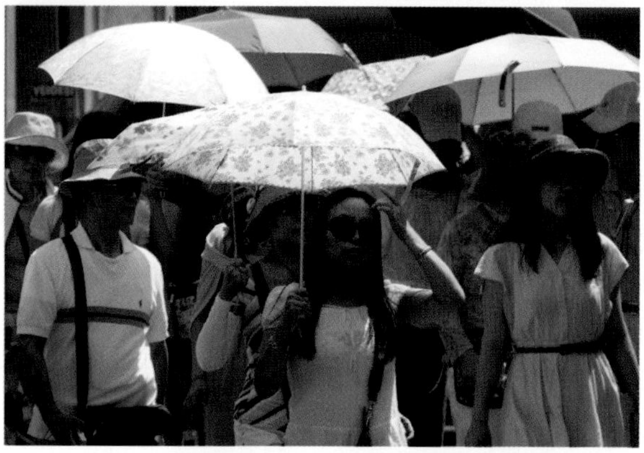

2. ______________________________

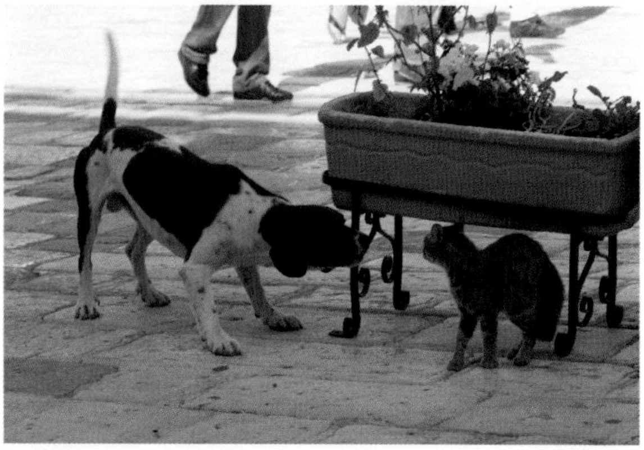

3. ______________________________

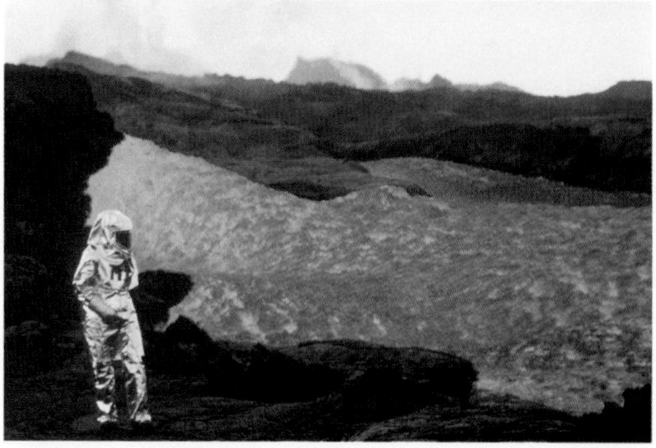

4. ______________________________

5. _____

_____

_____

_____

_____

_____

6. _____

_____

_____

_____

_____

_____

Writer's Note

Other Uses of _So_

One use of _so_ is as a connector in compound sentences to show a cause and result. However, _so_ has several other meanings.

In compound sentences, we use a comma with _so_, but we do <u>not</u> use a comma with the other uses of _so_.

Other Meanings of _So_	
Meaning	**Examples**
An adverb that means _very_ or _extremely_	It is **so** hot today. You speak English **so** well.
A connector that means _in order to_. The full form is _so that_. _So that_ is more formal than _so_, but the meaning is the same.	Lina went to the bank **so that** she could get some cash. Lina went to the bank **so** she could get some cash.
A common word at the beginning of a statement or question to continue a conversation. It is not used in academic writing.	Carlos: We were at the beach all day yesterday. Maria: **So** what time did you finally get home?

Use the picture and the prompts to write sentences. Use the present progressive tense. Then compare your sentences with a classmate's sentences.

Some fans / cheer / for their team

Other fans / wave / flags and banners

The coach / watch / the ball

The referee / run / toward the goal

The soccer ball / go / into the net

The forward / hope / the shot will be a goal

The goalkeeper / jump / for the ball

1. The soccer ball _____.

2. The goalkeeper _____.

3. The coach _____.

4. The referee _____.

5. The forward _____.

6. Some fans _____.

7. Other fans _____.

ACTIVITY 8 Writing a Paragraph

Rewrite the sentences from Activity 7 in paragraph form. Use your imagination and add some extra information to describe the game. Also, do the following:

- Use at least two adjectives.
- Make two compound sentences.
- Add a concluding sentence.
- Create a title for the paragraph.

Example Paragraph 3

_____

    The soccer game between Blackwatch and Dynamo is very exciting. Many things are

happening right now!

_____

_____

_____

_____

_____

_____

_____

_____

_____

Grammar for Writing

Verbs in Complex Sentences

When, while, before and *after* are connecting words that are commonly used to describe actions in the present in complex sentences.

- *While* can describe two actions that occur at the same time. You can use present progressive in each part of the sentence, or you can use present progressive in one clause and simple present in the other. There is no difference in meaning.

  Mark <u>is listening</u> to music **while** he <u>is surfing</u> the Internet.
  Mark <u>is listening</u> to music **while** he <u>surfs</u> the Internet.

- *When, after,* and *before* help describe the time order of activities in the present. The simple present tense (not present progressive) is most often used in both clauses.

  Mark <u>listens</u> to music **when** he <u>surfs</u> the Internet.
  After Mark <u>finishes</u> his homework, he <u>watches</u> television.
  Before Mark <u>goes</u> to bed, he <u>brushes</u> his teeth.

REMEMBER: When a connecting word begins the sentence, put a comma at the end of the clause. Do not use a comma when the connecting word is in the middle of the sentence.

Go back and look at your paragraph about the soccer game in Activity 8. Can you add a complex sentence to it?

ACTIVITY 9 **Practicing Complex Sentences in the Present**

Ask a partner the questions. Write his or her answers using a complex sentence. Use the appropriate connecting word.

1. What are you doing while you are sitting in class?

   _____

2. What do you usually do when you wake up?

   _____

3. After you eat breakfast in the morning, what do you do?

   _____

4. What do you do when you are not at school?

   _____

5. While you are completing your classwork, what is your teacher doing?

   _____

Identifying Sentence Types

Identify each sentence as a simple (*S*), compound (*CD*), or complex (*CX*) sentence. If the sentence is compound or complex, insert a comma where necessary.

1. ___S___ My brother and I are hiking and fishing this weekend.

2. ___CD___ The motorcycle is in the garage, and the car is in the driveway.

3. ___CX___ When Harry and Darlene went to the picnic yesterday, they got sunburns.

4. _____ I always think about my question before I ask the teacher.

5. _____ You are learning so many new words.

6. _____ A noun is a word like *sandwich* and a verb is an action word such as *eat*.

7. _____ While we are studying we are learning new material.

8. _____ After Kelly checks her e-mail she works for two hours.

9. _____ Lisana is working for a computer company but she does not have a computer engineering degree.

10. _____ I make a pot of coffee when I wake up in the morning.

11. _____ The capital of Argentina is Buenos Aires and it is the most populated city in the country.

12. _____ The traffic was terrible so Lance missed his plane.

Grammar for Writing

Adverbs of Manner

Adverbs are words that describe or give more information about verbs, adjectives, and other adverbs. There are several kinds of adverbs in English. **Adverbs of manner** usually describe verbs. They tell <u>how</u> an action is done.

> Kerry picked up the baby **carefully.**   (*How* did Kerry pick up the baby? **carefully**)

> My sister is studying **hard.**   (*How* is my sister studying? **hard**)

Adverbs of manner usually end in *-ly*.

Common Adverbs of Manner					
quickly	easily	nervously	carefully	happily	slowly
suddenly	quietly	badly	fast*	hard*	well*

*These adverbs do not use the *-ly* form.

Be careful! There are a few words that end in *–ly* that are adjectives, not adverbs.

> friendly   deadly   lovely   lonely

REMEMBER: Adjectives describe nouns. The baby is <u>happy</u>. Ben is a <u>happy</u> baby.

Go back and look at your paragraph about the soccer game. Can you add adverbs to describe the action?

ACTIVITY 11 Using Adverbs

Fill in each blank with an adverb that describes the action of the underlined verb. Use an adverb from the list of common adverbs of manner above or use your own.

1. Julia <u>is studying</u> _____ in the library.

2. He <u>got onto</u> the bus _____ because it was raining.

3. Mariah <u>spoke</u> _____ at the conference. Everyone was impressed by her speech.

4. David <u>is doing</u> _____ in this class. He never studies!

5. Nili <u>cried</u> very _____ during the movie. I didn't know she was crying until I looked at her.

6. Teresa <u>typed</u> the letter _____. I thought she would never finish.

7. Nate <u>read</u> the directions _____. He did not want to make a mistake.

8. I had a cold, so I <u>did not play</u> _____ at the soccer game last week.

9. Maria and Faisal <u>passed</u> the test _____ because they <u>studied</u> _____ for it.

10. Will <u>opened</u> the door _____ because he was afraid to wake up the baby.

Grammar for Writing

Prepositional Phrases of Place

A **prepositional phrase** is a phrase that begins with a preposition and includes a noun or pronoun. The noun or pronoun is called the **object of the preposition**.

prepositional phrase = preposition + object of preposition (noun / pronoun)

One type of prepositional phrase is the **prepositional phrase of place.** A prepositional phrase of place:

- tells about location—it answers the question *Where?*

- functions like an adverb—it modifies a verb

Parts of a Prepositional Phrase (of Place)				
Prepositional Phrase	**Preposition**	**Article** (*a, an, the*) **Demonstrative Determiner** (*this, that, these, those*) **Possessive Adjective** (*my, your, her,* etc.) **Quantifier** (*some, any, one, two,* etc.) **Ø**	**Adjective** Ø	**Noun** **Pronoun**
at the picnic	at	the		picnic
on that little table	on	that	little	table
next to my friends	next to	my		friends
under two old chairs	under	two	old	chairs
near them	near			them

It is common to put place phrases at the end of a sentence.

✗ We ate <u>at the picnic lots of salad</u>.

✓ We ate lots of salad at the picnic.

✗ Loretta <u>in my house lives</u>.

✓ Loretta lives in my house.

Prepositional Phrases of Place and Time Words

In sentences where you have a prepositional phrase of place <u>and</u> a time word or phrase, use this rule:

At the end of a sentence, place phrases usually come <u>before</u> time words or phrases.

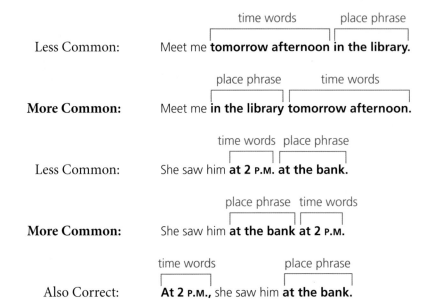

Less Common: | time words | place phrase |
Meet me **tomorrow afternoon in the library.**

More Common: | place phrase | time words |
Meet me **in the library tomorrow afternoon.**

Less Common: | time words | place phrase |
She saw him **at 2 P.M. at the bank.**

More Common: | place phrase | time words |
She saw him **at the bank at 2 P.M.**

Also Correct: | time words | place phrase |
At 2 P.M., she saw him **at the bank.**

ACTIVITY 12 **Practicing with Place Phrases and Time Words**

Unscramble the words to make correct sentences. Be sure to use the correct form of the verb. Use correct capitalization and punctuation.

1. Ashley / right now / drive / to the hospital

   _____

2. this semester / the Silva sisters / at City College / a grammar class / take

   _____

3. at the car dealership / today / a new car / we / buy

   _____

4. at the gym / exercise / Janie / this morning

   _____

5. we / take / today / in Mrs. Wang's class / an important test

   _____

6. put / Eric / right now / his books / in the trunk of his car

   _____

7. at the moment / eat dinner / Luis / at a restaurant

_____

8. Sara / a pie / now / put / in the oven

_____

9. I / at the moment / busy / be / at work

_____

10. the squirrels / now / nuts / bury / under our oak tree

_____

ACTIVITY 13 **Writing What You See: Describing Actions**

Write a paragraph based on observation. Choose a place to observe people—for example, a park, a mall, or a cafeteria. You may also use a show on television or an illustration in a magazine. Choose a situation or place that has several people who are doing different actions. Follow these instructions:

- Look at the people. What are they doing?
- Write about an object. What is happening with it?
- Use the connectors *and* and *so* if possible.
- Use one or two adverbs of manner.

There is a lot of action happening right now.

_____

_____

_____

_____

_____

_____

_____

_____

_____

_____

_____

ACTIVITY 14 **Editing: Grammar and Sentence Review**

Correct the paragraph. There are 13 mistakes.

2 compound sentence mistakes	2 capitalization mistakes	2 adverb mistakes
2 complex sentence mistakes	2 adjective mistakes	2 verb mistakes
1 mistake with time words		

Example Paragraph 4

The Squirrel

A small red squirrel climbing a tree. He is a young squirrel. His tail is twitching **nervously** and his nose is moving quick. I think he is searching for food. The squirrel red is right now on a long tree branch. He wants to jump to another tree. The squirrel hears something so he looks down. he is coming down from the tree tall. When he reaches the ground he runs to a few pieces of chocolate chip cookie. These cookie pieces lying on the grass. the squirrel is walking toward the food and **inspecting** it. The squirrel grabs the cookie and **stuffs** it in his mouth. While he is eating his tail is moving rapid. The little red squirrel is now happy.

nervously: in a worried or frightened way

to inspect: to look at carefully to learn more about it

to stuff: to quickly and carelessly put something into one's mouth

Building Better Vocabulary

ACTIVITY 15 **Word Associations**

Circle the word or phrase that is most closely related to the word or phrase on the left. If necessary, use a dictionary to check the meaning of words you do not know.

	A	B
1. remote	close	far
2. a site	an idea	a place
3. thirsty	to need food	to need water
4. to hear	with your ears	with your eyes
5. a carpet	a garage	a rug
6. steep	at an angle	flat
7. younger	18 years old	80 years old

	A	B
8. a mess	not organized	very organized
9. slippery	safe	unsafe
10. a piece	a coin	a part
11. to climb	to go near	to go up
12. a tail	a body part	a story
13. to inspect	to look at	to wait for
14. to stuff	to fill	to empty
15. empty	a lot inside	nothing inside

ACTIVITY 16 **Using Collocations**

Fill in each blank with the word that most naturally completes the phrase on the right. If necessary, use a dictionary to check the meaning of words you do not know.

1. line / step   to be in a _____

2. feel / have   to _____ very lucky

3. about / on   to be worried _____

4. delicious / dirty   to wash _____ clothes at the laundry

5. ancient / angle   to see an _____ site

6. picnic / sunburn   to get a _____

7. cleaner / machine   a vacuum _____

8. party / mess   to make a _____

9. monkey / room   an empty _____

10. nervous / powerful   to get _____ about something

ACTIVITY 17 Parts of Speech

Study the word forms. Fill in each blank with the best word form provided. Use the correct form of the verb. If necessary, use a dictionary to check the meaning of words you do not know. (NOTE: The word in bold is the original word that appears in the unit.)

Noun	Verb	Adjective	Sentence Practice
beauty	Ø	beautiful	1. I saw a _____ sunset yesterday.
			2. That painting is a thing of _____.
luck	Ø	**lucky**	3. The _____ lottery winner won $5 million.
			4. It was bad _____ that our team lost the game.
thirst	Ø	**thirsty**	5. If you are _____, drink some water.
			6. Keith is playing tennis. He is probably suffering from _____.
fishing	fish	Ø	7. _____ is a relaxing sport.
			8. We _____ in the lake behind our house.
hiking / **hiker** (A THING) / (A PERSON)	hike	Ø	9. The _____ carefully climbed up the steep trail.
			10. Ian _____ in the forest on the weekends.

Noun endings: *-ing, -er*
Adjective endings: *-ful, -y*

Original Student Writing

ACTIVITY 18 Original Writing Practice

Imagine that you are a TV news reporter. Right now you are at the location of an emergency situation (for example, a traffic accident, a building on fire, the scene of a natural disaster).

- Write a paragraph that describes what is happening.
- Use your imagination.
- You may use a picture from a newspaper, magazine, or the Internet to help your imagination.

Follow these steps for writing. Put a check (✓) next to each step as you complete it. When you finish your paragraph, use the checklist on the next page to edit your work.

_____ STEP 1: In your first sentence, tell where you are and what you are watching.

_____ STEP 2: In your next sentence, describe the person/people or thing(s) you see. Use adjectives to give a clear idea to your reader.

_____ STEP 3: In the next two to four sentences, describe what the people are doing.

_____ STEP 4: Use one or two adverbs in the sentences in STEP 3.

_____ STEP 5: Use *and* or *so* in one of the sentences. Remember to use a comma to separate the two clauses.

_____ STEP 6: Use a complex sentence with *when* or *while*.

_____ STEP 7: In the next sentence, write what you believe the people are thinking or feeling at this moment.

_____ STEP 8: In the final sentence, write your opinion about the situation.

_____ STEP 9: Use at least two of the vocabulary words or phrases presented in Activity 15, Activity 16, and Activity 17. Underline these words and phrases in your paragraph.

_____ STEP 10: Create a title for your work, and write it above the paragraph.

If you need ideas for words and phrases, see the Useful Vocabulary for Better Writing on pages 143-145.

☑ Checklist

1. ❑ I checked that each sentence has a subject and a verb.

2. ❑ I included two subjects and verbs (two clauses) in my compound sentences.

3. ❑ I used the present progressive verbs correctly.

4. ❑ I began every sentence with a capital letter.

5. ❑ I used commas correctly in compound and complex sentences.

6. ❑ I ended every sentence with the correct punctuation.

7. ❑ I gave my paragraph a title.

ACTIVITY 19 **Peer Editing**

Exchange papers from Activity 18 with a partner. Read your partner's paragraph. Then use Peer Editing Sheet 2 on ELTNGL.com/sites/els to help you comment on your partner's paragraph. Be sure to offer positive suggestions and comments that will help your partner improve his or her writing. Consider your partner's comments as you revise your own paragraph.

Additional Topics for Writing

Here are ten ideas for journal writing. Choose one or more of them to write about. Follow your teacher's directions. (We recommend that you skip a line after each line that you write. This gives your teacher a place to write comments.)

PHOTO
TOPIC: Look at the photo on pages 58–59. Imagine that you are in a large city like Tokyo, Toronto, London, Istanbul, or Seoul. Walk around the city and write down the things that you see. What is happening in this large city?

TOPIC 2: Watch several minutes of a television program. Describe what is happening in the show.

TOPIC 3: Describe how your life is now. Include your studies, your living arrangements, and your free time.

TOPIC 4: Imagine that you are a private investigator. Imagine that you are watching a specific character or person. Write down everything that the person is doing for five minutes.

TOPIC 5: Find a picture in a magazine. Choose a picture of many people who are doing different things. Describe what each person is doing.

TOPIC 6: Imagine that you are visiting the zoo. What are the other visitors doing? Write about what the different kinds of animals are doing.

TOPIC 7: Imagine that you are walking down the street, and you see your favorite movie star walk into a café. Follow this person. What is he/she doing?

TOPIC 8: Write a letter to your friend explaining what you are doing in this class. Tell about the assignments that you have and the writing skills that you are practicing.

TOPIC 9: If you have a pet, watch it closely for ten minutes. What is it doing? Where is it going? Is it playing? Jumping? Making noise?

TOPIC 10: Imagine that you are a news reporter for a movie magazine. You are at a famous awards ceremony. What are the people doing? Name some of the famous actors. (This word means male and female actors.) What are they doing? What are they wearing? What are they saying to their friends? What are they thinking?

Timed Writing

How quickly can you write in English? There are many times when you must write quickly, such as on a test. It is important to feel comfortable during those times. Timed-writing practice can make you feel better about writing quickly in English.

1. Take out a piece of paper.

2. Read the writing prompt below.

3. Brainstorm ideas for five minutes.

4. Write eight to ten sentences.

5. You have 20 minutes to write.

Describe an exciting (or boring, interesting, etc.) activity that you are doing this year. What is the activity? What are you doing to complete it? Give as many details as possible.

_____

_____

_____

_____

_____

_____

_____

_____

_____

A gargoyle looks down over the city and the Seine River in Paris, France.

OBJECTIVES **Grammar:** To learn about prepositions
Vocabulary and Spelling: To study common words with the sound of <u>o</u> in **hell<u>o</u>**
Writing: To write about things to see and do in your city

Can you write about things to see and do in your city?

Grammar for Writing

The man is **on** a mountain **in** Switzerland.

What Is a Preposition?

✓ **A preposition** is a word that shows the relationship between a noun and other words in the sentence.

✓ Common prepositions include:
   after   from   of   to   before   in   on   with

✓ A **prepositional phrase** is a preposition and its noun (or pronoun) object.

| prep + object | prep + object | prep + object |
| **after** my <u>class</u> | **in** <u>Japan</u> | **with** my <u>best friend</u> |

✓ Prepositions often answer **where, when,** or **how.**

where?	We live **in Tokyo.** Our apartment is **near a big park.**
when?	I was born **in 1992.** I was born **on May 2nd.**
how?	He likes to write **with a blue pen.** He likes to work **by himself.**

20 Prepositions You Need to Know*

1. of	What is the name **of** your book?	
2. to	I go **to** the park once a week.	
3. in	**PLACE:** We live **in** China. **TIME:** I was born **in** September.	
4. for	This clock is a gift **for** you.	
5. with	I go to the store **with** my mother.	
6. on	**PLACE:** The pencils are **on** the table. **TIME:** I work **on** Monday.	
7. at	**PLACE:** My sister works **at** Union Bank. **TIME:** She starts her job **at** 9 a.m.	
8. by	We live **by** the river.	
9. from	I am **from** San Francisco.	
10. up	This bus goes **up** that mountain.	
11. about	This story is **about** two people.	
12. than	Gold is more expensive **than** silver.	
13. after	We study **after** school.	
14. before	I usually go to sleep **before** midnight.	
15. down	She is walking **down** the steps.	
16. between	The United States is **between** Canada and Mexico.	
17. under	My shoes are **under** the sofa.	
18. since	I have worked here **since** 2010.	
19. without	My father likes coffee **without** sugar.	
20. near	I live **near** the beach.	

Based on the General Service List, Corpus of Contemporary American English, and other corpus sources.

ACTIVITY 1 **Finding Prepositional Phrases in Sentences**

Underline the 26 prepositional phrases in these sentences. Circle the prepositions.

My Student Life

1. I am a high school student (in) Singapore.

2. I go to Mayflower Secondary School.

3. I am in my last year at this school.

4. I begin my trip from home to school at 7 a.m.

5. My friends and I go to school by bus.

6. Our first class begins at 8 a.m.

7. My last class ends at 3 p.m.

8. After school, I take a bus to my house.

9. On the trip between my school and my house, I listen to music.

10. I eat dinner with my family at 7 p.m.

11. Before dinner, I usually study.

12. On Monday and Friday, I study from 4 p.m. to 7 p.m.

13. On some days, I study after dinner, too.

14. I study more on Monday than any other day.

at, on, in: Three Common Prepositions of Time

✓ Common prepositions of time are **at, on,** and **in**.

✓ You use **at** for clock time.

✓ You use **on** for days and dates.

✓ You use **in** for months, years, seasons, and longer periods of time.

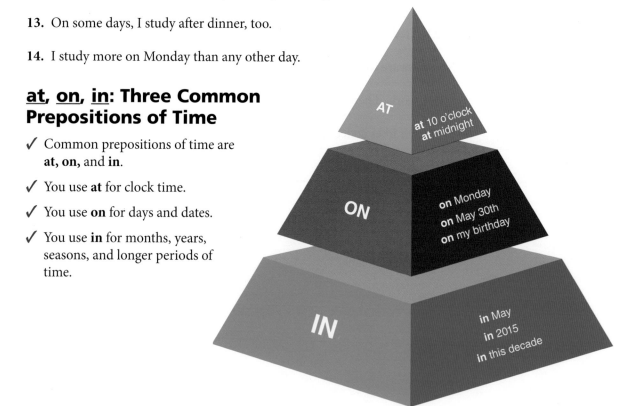

AT
at 10 o'clock
at midnight

ON
on Monday
on May 30th
on my birthday

IN
in May
in 2015
in this decade

ACTIVITY 2 **Prepositional Phrases of Time with at, on, in**

In A, write **at, on,** or **in** to complete the prepositional phrase of time. In B, write an original sentence with each prepositional phrase.

A.

1. _____ Monday   3. _____ midnight   5. _____ Friday   7. _____ January

2. _____ 9 o'clock   4. _____ 2012   6. _____ January 1st   8. _____ summer

B.

1. _____

2. _____

3. _____

4. _____

5. _____

6. _____

7. _____

8. _____

ACTIVITY 3 **at, on, in: Scrambled Sentences with Prepositional Phrases of Time**

Change the order of the words to write a correct sentence. Be careful with capital letters and punctuation.

1. at french o'clock 10 my begins class

   _____

2. at boston leaves the bus for nine

   _____

3. july family a my trip in takes

   _____

4. sunday show is on favorite our TV

   _____

5. maria and norah i 1985 born were in

   _____

6. birthday is in my january

_____

7. i go at sleep to midnight

_____

8. tuesday and have class english on monday wednesday we

_____

<u>at</u>, <u>on</u>, <u>in</u>: Three Common Prepositions of Place

✓ Common prepositions of place are **at, on,** and **in**.

✓ You use **at** for specific places, including addresses.

✓ You use **on** for streets.

✓ You use **in** for an area, a state, a country, a continent.

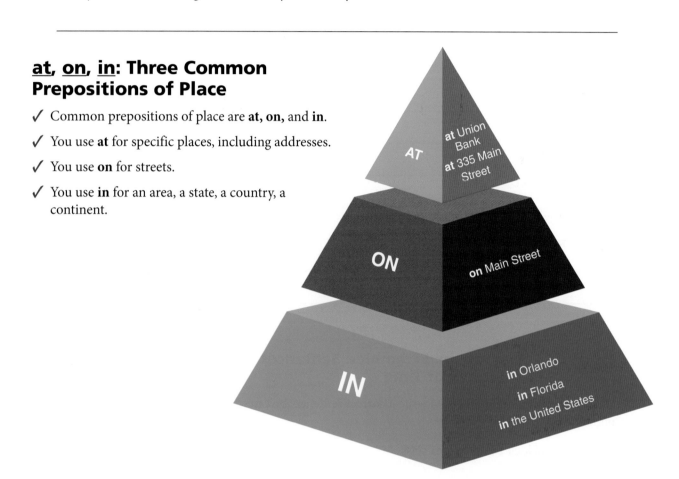

AT — at Union Bank, at 335 Main Street

ON — on Main Street

IN — in Orlando, in Florida, in the United States

ACTIVITY 4 **Prepositional Phrases of Place with <u>at</u>, <u>on</u>, <u>in</u>**

In A, write **at, on,** or **in** to complete the prepositional phrase of place. In B, write an original sentence with each prepositional phrase.

A.

1. _____ Union Bank

2. _____ Pine Street

3. _____ 277 Pine Street

4. _____ Los Angeles

5. _____ California

6. _____ the United States

7. _____ Minnesota University

8. _____ Shoes for Less

B.

1. _____
2. _____
3. _____
4. _____
5. _____
6. _____
7. _____
8. _____

ACTIVITY 5 Writing Two Related Sentences

Use the city and country in each item to write two sentences.

Step 1. In the first sentence, add the words **we live** to tell where you and your family live.

Step 2. In the second sentence, tell the location of the city. Use the words **is a city** in your sentence.

Be careful with capitalization, punctuation, articles, and prepositions.

1. athens – greece We live in Athens.   Athens is a city in Greece.

_____

2. osaka – japan _____

_____

3. rabat – morocco _____

_____

4. lima – peru _____

_____

5. seattle – united states _____

_____

6. dubai – united arab emirates _____

_____

7. chihuahua – mexico _____

_____

8. amsterdam – netherlands _____

_____

Write **at** or **on** to complete the prepositional phrase of place. Then write a sentence with the prepositional phrase to tell the location of the business on the map.

A Business Map of Downtown

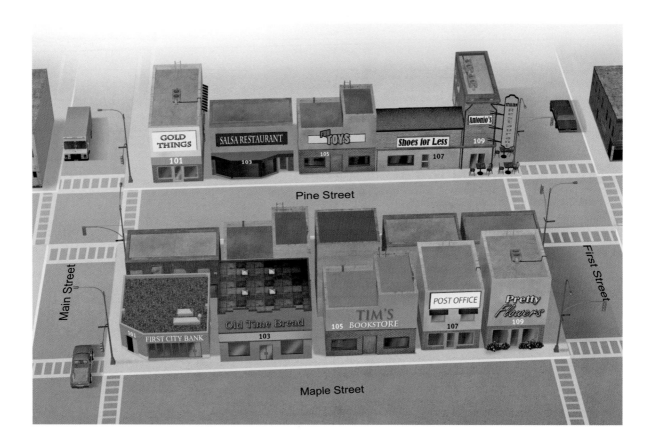

1. ___at___ 105 Maple Street   (Tim's Bookstore)

    Tim's Bookstore is at 105 Maple Street.

2. _____ Maple Street   (Pretty Flowers)

    _____

3. _____ Pine Street   (two restaurants)

    _____

4. _____ 101 Pine Street   (Gold Things)

    _____

5. _____ 101 Maple Street   (First City Bank)

    _____

6. _____ 107 Pine Street   (Shoes for Less)

_____

7. _____ Maple Street   (my bank and the post office)

_____

8. _____ Pine Street   (Gold Things, Fun Toys, Shoes for Less)

_____

Word Order: Place and Time in the Same Sentence

✓ When an English sentence has both a prepositional phrase of place and a prepositional phrase of time, you <u>usually</u> put **place before time**. (An easy way to remember this is **P comes before T** in the alphabet: <u>**P**lace before **T**ime.**)

Examples of Place before Time	
I go **to my office**. (place) I go **at 7 a.m.** (time)	place time I go **to my office** **at 7 a.m**.
He studies **at 8 o'clock**. (place) He studies **in the library**. (time)	place time He studies **in the library** **at 8 o'clock**.

ACTIVITY 7 **Scrambled Sentences with Prepositional Phrases of Place and Time**

Change the order of the words to write a correct sentence. Be careful with capital letters and punctuation.

1. we to went in london 1999

_____

2. supermarket saturday vegetables at mother on my buys the morning

_____

3. the the melissa library in at afternoon i and study

_____

4. one students lunch in from eat noon to the cafeteria o'clock

_____

5. want to i new study english in york in 2020

_____

6. in we to move apartment november will another

_____

Word Order: Beginning a Sentence with a Prepositional Phrase

✓ A sentence can begin with a prepositional phrase.

✓ You use a comma after a prepositional phrase that begins a sentence.

✓ You do not use a comma for prepositional phrases at the end of a sentence.

At the Beginning of the Sentence	At the End of the Sentence
In Japan, people drive on the left side of the road.	People drive on the left side of the road **in Japan.**
In April, Japanese students start school.	Japanese students start school **in April.**

✓ When writers begin a sentence with a prepositional phrase, they want to emphasize that information. The basic meaning is the same as when the prepositional phrase is near the end of the sentence.

ACTIVITY 8 **Writing Sentences that Start with Prepositional Phrases**

Write each sentence again. Move the last prepositional phrase to the beginning of your new sentence. Be careful with capitalization, word order, and punctuation.

1. My sister has English class on Monday.

   _____

2. Lynn, Jane, and Karen usually take bus 28 on Tuesday and Thursday.

   _____

3. You can see a better map of Asia.

   _____

4. Adjectives come before nouns in English.

   _____

5. Kevin and I have a very important meeting at 7 o'clock tonight.

   _____

6. U.S. citizens have to get a tourist visa for Russia, China, and Brazil.

   _____

Common Preposition Combinations after Verbs, Adjectives, and Nouns

✓ Sometimes a verb, an adjective, or a noun requires a certain preposition after it. You must memorize these word combinations.

Verbs		
	1. listen to	At night, I **listen to** music.
	2. look at	My brother likes to **look at** maps.
	3. look for	We will **look for** a new apartment.
	4. wait for	I **wait for** the bus here.

Adjectives		
	1. afraid of	They are **afraid of** snakes.
	2. different from	Chinese is **different from** Japanese.
	3. famous for	Paris is **famous for** the Eiffel Tower.
	4. far from	Alaska is **far from** Brazil.
	5. full of	This shopping center is **full of** teenagers on the weekend.
	6. happy about	We are very **happy about** your new job.
	7. important for	Eating good food is **important for** everyone.
	8. interested in	Are you **interested in** sports?
	9. married to	Lukas is **married to** Leila.
	10. necessary for	Water and light are **necessary for** plants to grow.
	11. ready for	We are **ready for** our trip to Spain.
	12. similar to	French is **similar to** Italian.
	13. sorry about	I am very **sorry about** your problems.
	14. tired of	The students are **tired of** tests every week.
	15. worried about	Mr. Miller is **worried about** his money problems.

Nouns		
	1. the cause of	No one knows **the cause of** the fire.
	2. the center of	The capital of the United States is not in **the center of** the country.
	3. the cost of	**The cost of** everything goes up every year.
	4. the difference between	Do you know **the difference between** a noun and a pronoun?
	5. an example of	*Kick* is **an example of** a word that begins and ends with the same letter.
	6. the matter with	What is **the matter with** you?
	7. the middle of	The horse is in **the middle of** the street.
	8. the price of	**The price of** food in that country is very expensive.
	9. a problem with	There is **a problem with** my phone.
	10. a question about	I have **a question about** my electricity bill.
	11. the same as	Your grade is **the same as** my grade.

ACTIVITY 9 **Practicing Prepositions after Verbs, Adjectives, and Nouns**

Underline the correct preposition in each sentence.

1. John is married (at, for, to, with) Beth.

2. Bolivia is an example (as, of, for, in) a country without a coast.

3. At my university, students spend a lot of time looking (at, for, in, of) a parking space.

4. We will wait (by, for, out, to) you right here. Please come back quickly.

5. I am ready (in, from, for, on) my big test tomorrow.

6. Pink is similar (at, for, in, to) red.

7. Green is different (at, for, from, to) red.

8. I do not want to have a problem (of, for, in, with) my visa.

9. I like to listen (for, in, on, to) music in my car.

10. We like sports. We are very interested (of, in, on, with) European and South American soccer.

Common Student Mistakes

Student Mistake **X**	Problem	Correct Example **✓**
Miami and Orlando are **on** Florida.	wrong preposition	Miami and Orlando are **in** Florida.
I like to **listen music** in my car.	preposition missing	I like to listen **to** music in my car.
Ed goes **on Tuesdays and Thursdays to his classes**.	time before place	Ed goes **to his classes on Tuesdays and Thursdays.**
With my friend I went to the beach last weekend.	comma missing after prepositional phrase that begins a sentence	With my friend**,** I went to the beach last weekend.

ACTIVITY 10 **Scrambled Sentences**

Change the order of the words to write a correct sentence. Be careful with spelling, capital letters, punctuation, and word order.

Comparing Three Long Flights from New York

1. schedules are long for three the flights these

_____

2. these on three all international airlines of are flights

_____

3. from number new york goes 434 to flight london

_____

4. and 8 a.m. leaves it at it 8 p.m. arrives

_____

5. goes york 221 flight tokyo to number new from

_____

6. arrives the 3:30 p.m. at leaves this next 11:30 a.m. at flight day one and

_____

7. lima 395 goes new from flight to york

_____

8. at arrives it 8 p.m. and 9 a.m. at leaves

_____

9. stops hours in this panama two flight for

_____

ACTIVITY 11 **Finding and Correcting 10 Mistakes**

Circle the ten mistakes. Then write the sentences correctly. The number in parentheses ( ) is the number of mistakes in that sentence. Be ready to explain your answers.

Things I Want To Do

1. I am student at Washington High School. (1)

_____

2. My class favorite is the geography. (2)

_____

3. In the future I want to visit the pyramids near from Cairo in Egypt. (2)

_____

4. I want to walk up a mountain at Chile. (1)

_____

5. I want to see the buildings famous at Paris. (2)

_____

6. After Paris I want to go Japan to ride on the fast trains there. (2)

_____

Track 7 •)) **ACTIVITY 12** **Dictation**

You will hear six sentences three times. Listen carefully and write the six sentences. The number in parentheses ( ) is the number of words. Be careful with capital letters and end punctuation.

1. _____ (7)

2. _____ (7)

3. _____ (8)

4. _____ (9)

5. _____ (11)

6. _____ (10)

Practicing Grammar and Vocabulary in Model Writing

Read the sentences in the paragraph very carefully. Fill in the missing words from the word bank. Circle the 24 letters that need to be capital letters. Then copy the paragraph on your own paper.

than	of	on	in	from	at
in	and	in	with	for	also

Tourists in Paris

1 marie lives _____ an apartment in paris. **2** her apartment is

_____ the tenth floor of a very big apartment building. **3** _____ her

apartment, she can see paris well. **4** _____ example, her apartment is near the eiffel

tower. **5** every year more _____ fifteen million tourists come to paris.

6 most tourists visit _____ the summer. **7** it is difficult to find a good hotel room

_____ july. **8** they come _____ a long list of things to do in paris.

9 many people like to take a picture _____ the eiffel tower. **10** they _____

like to visit the many old buildings in the city. **11** some tourists look _____ the famous

paintings in the louvre museum. **12** tourists love paris, _____ marie loves her city, too.

ACTIVITY 14 **Guided Writing: Making Changes in Model Writing**

Write the paragraph from Activity 13 again, but make the changes listed below and all other necessary changes.

<u>Sentence 1</u>. Change **Paris** to a different city that tourists like to visit. You will also need to make this change in several other places.

<u>Sentence 1</u>. Change **Marie** to a male name that is popular in your new city. You will need to change this name and the possessive adjective **her** to **his** in several other places.

<u>Sentences 4 and 9.</u> Change **the Eiffel Tower** to a famous location in your new city.

<u>Sentences 5, 6, 7.</u> Change the number and the months. Use correct information about your new city.

<u>Sentences 9, 10, 11.</u> Change to information about your new city.

_____

_____

_____

_____

_____

_____

_____

_____

_____

_____

_____

_____

Building Vocabulary and Spelling

Learning Words with the Sound of o in hello *

o = h e l l o   This sound is usually spelled with the letters **o, o +**
consonant + final **e, ow, oa, old, oe**, and another spelling.

phone

boat

ACTIVITY 15 **Which Words Do You Know?**

This list has 52 common words with the sound of **o** in hell**o**.

1. Notice the spelling patterns.

2. Check ✓ the words you know.

3. Look up new words in a dictionary. Write the meanings in your Vocabulary Notebook.

Common Words

GROUP 1:
Words spelled with **o**

☐ 1. a g o
☐ 2. a l s o
☐ 3. b o t h
☐ 4. g o
☐ 5. h e l l o
☐ 6. h o t e l
☐ 7. m o s t
☐ 8. n o b o d y
☐ 9. N o v e m b e r
☐ 10. o c e a n

☐ 11. O c t o b e r
☐ 12. o n l y
☐ 13. o p e n
☐ 14. s o

GROUP 2:
Words spelled with **o +**
consonant + final **e**

☐ 15. a l o n e
☐ 16. c l o s e
☐ 17. c l o t h e s

☐ 18. h o m e
☐ 19. h o p e
☐ 20. j o k e
☐ 21. n o s e
☐ 22. n o t e
☐ 23. p h o n e
☐ 24. s m o k e
☐ 25. s t o v e
☐ 26. t e l e p h o n e

*List is from: Spelling Vocabulary List © 2013 Keith Folse

GROUP 3:
Words that end in **ow**

- [ ] 27. b e l o w
- [ ] 28. f o l l o w
- [ ] 29. g r o w
- [ ] 30. k n o w
- [ ] 31. l o w
- [ ] 32. o w n
- [ ] 33. s h o w
- [ ] 34. s l o w
- [ ] 35. s n o w
- [ ] 36. t o m o r r o w
- [ ] 37. w i n d o w
- [ ] 38. y e l l o w

GROUP 4:
Words spelled with **oa** (in the middle of the word)

- [ ] 39. b o a t
- [ ] 40. c o a c h
- [ ] 41. c o a s t
- [ ] 42. c o a t
- [ ] 43. g o a l
- [ ] 44. r o a d
- [ ] 45. s o a p

GROUP 5:
Words that end in **old**

- [ ] 46. c o l d
- [ ] 47. g o l d

- [ ] 48. o l d
- [ ] 49. t o l d

GROUP 6:
Words spelled with **oe**

- [ ] 50. g o e s
- [ ] 51. t o e

GROUP 7:
Other spelling

- [ ] 52. a l t h o u g h

ACTIVITY 16 **Matching Words and Pictures**

Use the list in Activity 15 to write the common word that matches the picture.

1. _____   3. _____

2. _____   4. _____

5. _____   7. _____

6. _____   8. _____

ACTIVITY 17 **Spelling Words with the Sound of <u>o</u> in hell<u>o</u>**

Fill in the missing letters to spell words with the sound of <u>o</u> in hell<u>o</u>. Then copy the correct word.

1. bel __   _____   7. __ n   _____

2. kn __   _____   8. Oct __ ber   _____

3. c __ t   _____   9. h __ p __   _____

4. g __ s   _____   10. al __ n __   _____

5. __ ld   _____   11. alth __   _____

6. b __ th   _____   12 c __ st   _____

Complete each sentence with the correct word from Activity 17. Then copy the sentence with correct capital letters and punctuation.

1. the month between september and november is _____

_____

2. how _____ are your grandparents

_____

3. we really _____ that it does not rain tomorrow

_____

4. a score _____ 70 on this exam is not good

_____

5. _____ el salvador and costa rica are in central america

_____

6. air canada 227 _____ from toronto to atlanta

_____

7. very few people _____ the capital of malaysia

_____

8. she passed the test _____ she did not study a lot

_____

9. everyone wears a heavy _____ in the middle of winter

_____

10. how many cell phones do you _____

_____

11. kevin lives _____

_____

12. countries such as bolivia sudan laos and mongolia do not have a _____

_____

Scrambled Letters

Change the order of the letters to make a word that has the sound of <u>o</u> in hell<u>o</u>.

_____	**1.** p e n o	_____	**8.** m t o s
_____	**2.** e k o j	_____	**9.** y e k b a o r d
_____	**3.** p h n e o t e e l	_____	**10.** o s
_____	**4.** s l o c e	_____	**11.** s o n e
_____	**5.** l o n y	_____	**12.** o g a
_____	**6.** c c o a h	_____	**13.** h o w s
_____	**7.** w o l s	_____	**14.** n o y d o b

Track 8 ◉))) **ACTIVITY 20** **Spelling Practice**

Write the word that you hear. You will hear each word two times.

1._____	6._____	11._____
2._____	7._____	12._____
3._____	8._____	13._____
4._____	9._____	14._____
5._____	10._____	15._____

ACTIVITY 21 **Spelling Review: Which Word Is Correct?**

This review covers the different ways of spelling <u>o</u> in hell<u>o</u> in this unit. Read each pair of words. Circle the word that is spelled correctly.

	A	B		A	B
1.	oshun	ocean	**11.**	tomorrow	tomorow
2.	ownly	only	**12.**	gole	goal
3.	below	beloe	**13.**	coald	cold
4.	folow	follow	**14.**	alown	alone
5.	know	knoe	**15.**	clothes	closse
6.	also	alsow	**16.**	joke	joake
7.	ago	agoa	**17.**	smoughk	smoke
8.	helo	hello	**18.**	althow	although
9.	own	oun	**19.**	sough	so
10.	slowe	slow	**20.**	goes	gose

Read the four words in each row. Underline the word that is spelled correctly.

	A	B	C	D
1.	bothe	bouth	both	bouthe
2.	moni	muney	mney	money
3.	jome	ome	home	phome
4.	usually	yusually	uselly	usualy
5.	soap	sope	soop	sowp
6.	most	moast	mowst	moest
7.	gaym	gaim	game	guame
8.	althoh	althow	althoe	although
9.	number	nimbr	nummber	nombour
10.	oppen	open	oben	obben
11.	buthir	boter	boather	bother
12.	nobember	Nobember	november	November
13.	belo	below	billew	beloe
14.	tomorrow	tomorow	tommorow	tommorrow
15.	trabel	truvel	travel	trubel
16.	imbossible	impossible	imposibl	empossible
17.	encide	inseed	incide	inside
18.	goale	gole	gol	goal
19.	necesary	necessary	nessesery	nessesary
20.	kno	knoe	knou	know

Original Student Writing

Writing Your Ideas in Sentences or a Paragraph

Write eight to twelve sentences on your own paper. Imagine that you live in a city that millions of tourists visit each year. Write about your city. What do tourists come to see there? When do they come there? What advice can you give them about things to see and do in that city? Use prepositions of place and time.

For help, you can follow the examples in Activity 13 (page 97) and Activity 14 (page 98).

Peer Editing

Exchange papers from the above activity. Read your partner's sentences. Then use Peer Editing Sheet 3 on ELTNGL.com/sites/els to make comments about the writing.

PREPARING TO READ

BUILDING
VOCABULARY

A Use the words in **blue** to complete the sentences.

> anywhere   trip   hiked   important

1. She took a _____ to London.

2. Last weekend, I _____ in the mountains.

3. You can sit here, there, or _____ .

4. It is _____ to study for the test!

BUILDING
VOCABULARY

B Read the questions. Choose the correct answers.

1. What does a **map** give?
   a. directions   b. news

2. What can you **choose**?
   a. your parents   b. your friends

3. What can you **climb**?
   a. a chair   b. a hill

4. Which is an **adventure**?
   a. sleeping late   b. going to a new place

USING
VOCABULARY

C Circle the answer that is true for you. If you answer *Yes*, write a place to complete the sentence.

1. Do you hike?   Yes / No

   I hike in _____ .

2. Do you ever mountain climb?   Yes / No

   I mountain climb in _____ .

3. Do you ever go on adventures?   Yes / No

   I went on an adventure in _____ .

What are some adventures you can have close to home?

Alastair Humphreys sleeps on a hill during a microadventure.

ADVENTURES ANYWHERE •))) Track 9

Alastair Humphreys is a British adventurer. Humphreys rode his bike around the world. He also rowed a boat from Africa to South America. In 2011, he had some big **adventures** – and did not leave the United Kingdom.

For a year, Humphreys went on microadventures. These are small trips close to home. Humphries explains: "I started to think that it was possible to have an adventure **anywhere**." For his first trip, he **hiked** around the M25 with a friend. The M25 is a 188-kilometer road. It goes all around London. He also swam in the River Thames and went on a mountain biking **trip**. Humphreys learned something **important**: We find adventure by trying something new.

Humphreys wanted other people to learn this, too. So he asked people to go on microadventures and to take short videos of their trips. He asked them to do things like **climb** a hill, or **choose** any place on a **map** and go there. People around the world went on microadventures. They posted their videos on Twitter.

Try a Microadventure Yourself

Here are six ideas. Why not try one? As Humphreys says, "Life is now or never. Fill it with adventure!"

- Climb a hill that you can see from your town.
- Sleep in your garden for a night.
- Go on a journey to an island.
- Choose a river and travel to where it starts.
- Travel to the coast and sleep there for a night.
- Take a friend on their first microadventure.

UNDERSTANDING THE READING

UNDERSTANDING
MAIN IDEAS

A Circle the two main ideas of the text.

1. Humphreys went on big adventures.

2. Small trips can be adventures.

3. People around the world went on microadventures.

4. We find adventure by trying something new.

UNDERSTANDING
DETAILS

B Complete the sentences with the correct answers.

1. Alastair Humphreys is _____.
   a. African   b. South American   c. British

2. Humphreys' first microadventure was _____.
   a. hiking the M25 in London
   b. riding his bike around the world
   c. rowing from Africa to South America

3. Humphreys asked people to take _____ their microadventures.
   a. pictures of   b. videos of   c. notes about

4. People posted their videos on _____.
   a. Twitter   b. Facebook   c. Tumblr

5. Humphreys says: *Life is now or never. Fill it with* _____.
   a. hiking   b. trips   c. adventure

EXPANDING
UNDERSTANDING

C Read the questions. Then discuss with a partner.

1. Look at the six microadventures ideas on page 107. Which ones do you want to try? Why? Which ones do you *not* want to try? Why not?

2. Think of another microadventure and write about it. Explain where it is and what you can do.

PREPARING TO READ

A   Use the words in **blue** to complete the sentences.

> capital   tour   museum

1. We went to the _____ to see art.

2. The _____ of China is Beijing.

3. We went on a _____ of the city to see famous places.

B   Read the sentences. Look at the word in **blue**. Choose the word that has the same meaning.

1. I love my new phone. It's **amazing**.

   a.   great   b.   ok

2. We can walk to the café. It's **nearby**.

   a.   far away   b.   close

3. I don't go to concerts. I don't like to be with **crowds**.

   a.   few people   b.   many people

C   Complete the information to make sentences about you.

1. The capital of my country is _____.

2. A museum I visited is _____.

3. A restaurant nearby is _____.

4. Imagine a tour of your town. Where should the tour stop? Write a list of places:

   _____   _____

   _____   _____

   _____   _____

Guards march outside Buckingham Palace.

Actors attend a premiere of the movie *Arrival* in Leicester Square.

A MOVIE-GOER'S GUIDE TO LONDON •))) Track 10

London is the setting[1] for many popular movies. Are you visiting the **capital** of the UK? Follow this walking **tour** to see interesting places connected to movies.

Start at ❶ **the London Film Museum**. You can see items from many famous movies here. The **museum** is near Covent Garden—a famous market. And while you're there, watch some of the **amazing** street performers.

Next, walk down King Street. Then go along New Row to ❷ **J Sheekey**. You may see TV and movie stars at this restaurant. And it's not too expensive. You can get a great meal for under £25.

Nearby is ❸ **Leicester Square**. The London Film Festival is in this square. One of the exits of the underground station is in the movie *Harry Potter and the Half-Blood Prince*.

To get away from the **crowds**, go to ❹ **Leicester Square Gardens**. There is a statue of William Shakespeare here. Shakespeare wrote his most famous plays in London. Many of his plays later became movies.

From Leicester Square, walk down to Charing Cross Road and then to ❺ **the National Gallery**. You can see famous paintings by artists like Vincent van Gogh and Leonardo da Vinci here. This museum was in the James Bond movie *Skyfall*.

Finally, go south on Charing Cross Road, and follow the Mall. At the end of it, look for ❻ **Buckingham Palace**. This is the home of the British royal family. The palace is in a few movies, such as *The BFG* and *The King's Speech*.

[1] A **setting** is a place where something happens.

UNDERSTANDING THE READING

A What is the writer's purpose? Circle the best answer.

UNDERSTANDING PURPOSE

1. to tell about the most famous places in London

2. to tell about how to follow a map

3. to tell about interesting places in London connected to movies

B Match each place with what is there.

UNDERSTANDING DETAILS

1. Buckingham Palace   a. TV and movie stars

2. Leicester Square   b. street performers

3. Covent Garden   c. famous paintings

4. J Sheekey   d. the British royal family

5. The National Gallery   e. statue of William Shakespeare

C Imagine you are going to London. Put a check (✓) next to three things you most want to see. Then compare and discuss your choices with a partner or write sentences about yourself. Did your partner choose the same places?

EXPANDING UNDERSTANDING

Use this sentence frame: *I want to go to _____ because _____.*

I want to go to Covent Garden because I like street performers.

I / My partner wants to go to…	Me	My Partner
1. The London Film Museum		
2. J Sheekey		
3. Leicester Square		
4. Leicester Square Gardens		
5. The National Gallery		
6. Buckingham Palace		

PREPARING TO READ

BUILDING
VOCABULARY

A Use the words in **blue** to complete the sentences.

> photo   contact   click on   users

1. That website has one million _____.

2. _____ that link with your mouse.

3. Look at this _____ of my sister.

4. You can _____ your teacher at this email address.

BUILDING
VOCABULARY

B Read the questions. Choose the correct answers.

1. What can you **post**?
   a. a photo
   b. a pizza

2. Which is a **hobby**?
   a. studying
   b. playing guitar

3. How do babies **communicate**?
   a. they cry
   b. they eat

4. Which can you **join**?
   a. a group
   b. a computer

USING
VOCABULARY

C Complete the information to make sentences about you.

1. I have a hobby. I like to _____.

2. The last website or app I joined is _____.

3. The last thing I posted was _____.

Photos like this, of a surfer in California, have helped Chris Burkard gain a huge following on Instagram.

SHARING SUCCESS ·)) Track 11

Photography was not just a **hobby** for Chris Burkard. It was his job. His amazing **photos** made him successful. But in 2013, something happened that made him more successful.

Burkard was on a photography trip in Iceland. A surfer showed him a photo-sharing app. It was called Instagram. Burkard **joined**. He started **posting** photos. In four years, he had over 2 million followers.

Photo-sharing sites like Instagram, Imgur, and Flickr are getting more and more popular. In 2011, Instagram had 5 million **users**. By 2016, it had 500 million. These sites help photographers like Burkard connect with a large number of people.

How do you make a successful photo-sharing account? Here are some tips.

1. **Be yourself.** Don't try to be like anyone else. Create your own style.

2. **Get connected.** Share photo-sharing posts on other social media sites. People may see your posts. Then they may **click on** them and go to your photo-sharing account.

3. **Choose hashtags carefully.** Use popular hashtags. For example, many people use the hashtag #getoutside for photos of the outdoors. There are about 6 million Instagram photos with the hashtag. Use it, and people may look for this hashtag and find you.

4. **Contact other people.** Follow and comment on other people's posts. Then they may comment on your posts.

5. **Communicate with your followers.** Make them feel like part of a community. For example, ask questions, and share your ideas.

UNDERSTANDING THE READING

UNDERSTANDING
MAIN IDEAS

A Circle the main idea of the text.

1. Chris Burkard has two million followers on Twitter.

2. Photo-sharing sites are getting more and more popular.

3. Photo-sharing sites help photographers connect to many people.

IDENTIFYING
EXAMPLES

B Read the sentences. Choose the correct answers to complete the sentences.

1. Photo-sharing sites like _____ are getting more and more popular.
   a. Instagram, Imgur, and Flickr
   b. Facebook and Twitter

2. Use popular hashtags. For example, many people use the hashtag _____ for photos of the outdoors.
   a. #getoutside
   b. #livelife

3. Make your followers feel like part of a community. For example, _____ and share your ideas.
   a. ask questions
   b. say "hello"

EXPANDING
UNDERSTANDING

C Complete each of the sentences. Then discuss your answers with a partner or write sentences.

Imagine you are signing up for an Instagram account to share photos.

1. I will share photos of _____.

2. I will use the hashtag #_____.

3. I will also share my photos on _____. (other social media)

4. I think I will have _____ followers in a year. (number)

PREPARING TO READ

A   Use the words in **blue** to complete the sentences.

> appeared   direction   guess   believe

1. I don't think that story is true. I don't _____ it.
2. How old am I? Try to _____.
3. After the rain, a rainbow _____ in the sky.
4. The noise is coming from the _____ of that building.

B   Read the questions. Choose the correct answers.

1. Which is **real**?
   a. Santa Claus   b. the queen of England
2. Which is a **prize**?
   a. money   b. a birthday present
3. What does **missing** mean?
   a. here   b. not here

C   Complete the information to make sentences about you.

1. I guess there are _____ people in this city. (number)
2. I once won a prize for _____.
3. Who appears in many of your photos?_____.

IS IT REAL? •))) Track 12

Look at the two shark photos on this page. One is **real**. The other is fake[1]. Can you tell which is which?

In 2016, an amazing photo **appeared** on Twitter. It showed a great white shark jumping out of the water. The photo went viral[2]. Who posted the photo? The person used the name Bob Burton. He said he was National Geographic's best photographer. He said the photo was National Geographic's photo of the year.

None of this was true. There is no Bob Burton at National Geographic. They have no **prize** for photo of the year. And the photo was not real. Someone made it on a computer.

Computer technology and social media make it easier to make and share fake photos. So how do you know if a photo is real? First, look for a source. Where does the photo come from? Is there a photographer's name? Is

there information about them on the Internet? Second, look for clues in the photo. Sometimes the light is wrong. Maybe the **direction** of the light is wrong. Is anything in the photo too big or too small? Is anything **missing**?

Did you **guess** correctly? The fake photo is on the left. Look closely. Something in the photo is not right. The water doesn't look natural. The light also looks a little too bright. But the photo on the right is real. Chris Fallows took this photo. Fallows is a photographer. He spends a lot of time taking photos of sharks. He waited in his boat for a day to get this photo.

New technology is changing how we make and share photos. But don't **believe** everything you see!

[1] If something is **fake**, it is not real.
[2] If something goes **viral**, it spreads on the Internet very quickly.

UNDERSTANDING THE READING

A Which is the best title for this passage?

UNDERSTANDING GIST

1. National Geographic's Best Shark Photos

2. Famous Photos on the Internet

3. Don't Believe Everything You See

B Read the questions. Choose the correct answers.

UNDERSTANDING DETAILS

1. Where did the photo of the shark appear?

   a. a newspaper   b. Twitter   c. Facebook

2. What clue can tell you that a photo is fake?

   a. the light is wrong   b. the photo is too big   c. the photo is black and white

3. Which photo is fake?

   a. the one on the right   b. the one on the left   c. both of them

4. Who took the real photo?

   a. National Geographic   b. Bob Burton   c. Chris Fallows

C Circle an answer to each question. Then discuss your answers with a partner or write answers.

EXPANDING UNDERSTANDING

1. Which photo did you guess was real?   The left / The right

2. Was your guess correct?   Yes / No

3. Will you look at photos on social media differently now?   Yes / No

4. Tell your partner about a fake photo you saw recently. Then write sentences about it.

VOCABULARY EXTENSION   UNIT 1

WORD PARTNERS noun + *trip*

Collocations are words that often go together, such as *business trip*. Some collocations are in the noun + noun form. Here are some common collocations with the noun *trip*.

business trip: a trip taken as part of someone's job

road trip: a long trip by car or motorcycle

fishing trip: a trip to go fishing

field trip: a trip to study something

A Complete each sentence with the correct form of the collocations from the box above.

1. Next week, the school students are going on a _____ to the science museum.

2. A sales representative goes on many _____ to see customers far away.

3. I'm going on a _____ this weekend to try and catch some tuna.

4. My friend and I are going on a _____ through Europe next year. We're driving from Paris to Moscow.

WORD WEB Prepositions of Place and Direction

Prepositions of place describe where things are.

*The library is **near** the town hall.*

*I parked my car **between** two buses.*

*They sat **opposite** each other at dinner.*

Prepositions of direction describe how things move. Prepositions of direction usually modify a verb of movement.

*He walked **across** the road.*

*I flew **over** India on my way to Europe.*

*You need to drive **through** a long tunnel to get there.*

B Circle the best preposition to complete each sentence.

1. To get to Manhattan, you can go **through** / **over** the Brooklyn Bridge.

2. The world-famous Times Square is **between** / **through** 42nd and 47th Streets. The Empire State Building is **near** / **across** Times Square.

3. My office is directly **opposite** / **between** the Empire State Building.

4. Many tourists like walking **opposite** / **through** Central Park.

VOCABULARY EXTENSION   UNIT 3

WORD PARTNERS *verb + photo*

Here are some common verb + noun collocations with the noun *photos*.

edit *a photo*: to fix a photo using a computer (e.g. brightening the image)

download *a photo*: to move a photo from a camera to a computer

upload *a photo*: to move a photo from a computer to a website

share *a photo*: to show a photo to a group of friends online

print *a photo*: to produce a copy of a photo on a machine

A Circle the best word to complete each sentence.

1. During my trip to London, I **printed** / **took** hundreds of photos of the city and **uploaded** / **took** them to my Facebook page.

2. My internet connection was slow, so it took a long time to **print** / **download** the photo.

3. I **share** / **edit** all my photos with my friends online.

4. I **downloaded** / **printed** a photo of my family and put it on my wall.

WORD FORMS Nouns and Verbs with the Same Spelling

Some words can be spelled in the same way as both nouns and verbs. For example, *guess* (the noun) is spelled the same way as *guess* (the verb).

VERB

*Can you **guess** which photo is fake?*

NOUN

My best **guess** is this photo is fake.

B Read the sentences below. Write **N** for noun or **V** for verb above each underlined word.

1. A photographer <u>dreams</u> of taking the perfect picture.

2. Taking photos on top of Mount Everest involves a long and difficult <u>climb</u>.

3. It was a silly <u>plan</u> to post a fake photograph online.

4. Many people <u>contact</u> friends using online social media.

5. I use my <u>phone</u> to post photos online.

EDITING CHECKLIST

Use the checklist to find errors in your writing task for each unit.

	WRITING TASK	
	1	2
1. Is the first word of every sentence capitalized?		
2. Does every sentence end with the correct punctuation?		
3. Does every sentence contain a subject and a verb?		
4. Do your subjects and verbs agree?		
5. Do all possessive nouns have an apostrophe?		
6. Are all proper nouns capitalized?		
7. Is the spelling of places, people, and other proper nouns correct?		

Brief Writer's Handbook

The Parts of a Paragraph

What Is a Paragraph?

A **paragraph** is a group of sentences about **one** specific topic. A paragraph usually has three to ten sentences.

A paragraph is indented. This means there is a white space at the beginning of the first sentence.

Here is a group of sentences that can also be a paragraph.

Sentences	Paragraph
1. I have a big family.	indent ↓
2. My name is Anna Sanders.	I have a big family. My name is Anna Sanders. I am twenty
3. I am twenty years old.	years old. I study English at my school. I have two brothers. I also
4. I study English at my school.	have two sisters. I love my brothers and sisters a lot. We are a very
5. I have two brothers.	happy family.
6. I also have two sisters.	
7. I love my brothers and sisters a lot.	
8. We are a very happy family.	

Parts of a Paragraph

A paragraph has three main parts: the topic sentence, the body, and a concluding sentence. See the example below that shows these parts.

1. **The Topic Sentence**

   Every good paragraph has a **topic sentence**. The topic sentence tells the main idea of the whole paragraph.

   The topic sentence:

   - is usually the first sentence in the paragraph.
   - should not be too specific or too general.

   If a paragraph does not have a topic sentence, the reader may not know what the paragraph is about. Make sure every paragraph has a topic sentence.

2. The Body

Every good paragraph must have sentences that support the topic sentence. These supporting sentences are called the **body** of a paragraph.

The supporting sentences:

- give more information, such as details or examples, about the topic sentence.

- must be related to the topic sentence.

A good body can make your paragraph stronger. You must be sure to cut out any unrelated or unconnected ideas.

3. The Concluding Sentence

In addition to a topic sentence and body, every good paragraph has a **concluding sentence**. This sentence ends the paragraph with a final thought.

The concluding sentence:

- can give a summary of the information in the paragraph.

- can give information that is similar to the information in the topic sentence.

- can give a suggestion, an opinion, or a prediction.

topic sentence   the body

I have a big family. My name is Anna Sanders. I am twenty years old. I study English at

my school. I have two brothers. I also have two sisters. I love my brothers and sisters a lot.

concluding sentence (opinion)

We are a very happy family.

Read each paragraph and answer the questions that follow.

The Best Place to Relax

My back **porch** is my favorite place to **relax**. First, it has lots of comfortable chairs with soft pillows. I feel so good when I sit in them. My back porch is also very peaceful. I can sit and think there. I can even read a great book and nobody **bothers** me. Finally, in the evening, I can sit on my porch and watch the sunset. Watching the beautiful colors always calms me. I can relax in many places, but my back porch is the best.

a porch: a part at the front or back of a house with only a floor and a roof

to relax: to rest or do something enjoyable

to bother: to make someone feel worried or upset

1. How many sentences are in this paragraph? _____

2. What is the main topic of this paragraph? (Circle.)

    a. The writer likes watching the sunset.

    b. The writer likes to read a book in a quiet place.

    c. The writer likes to relax on her back porch.

3. What is the first sentence of this paragraph? (This is the topic sentence.) Write it here.

    _____

    _____

4. The writer gives examples of how her porch is relaxing. List the four things the writer does to relax on her porch.

    a. _____The writer sits in comfortable chairs._____

    b. _____

    c. _____

    d. _____

5. Read the paragraph again. Find at least two adjectives and write them below.

    _____

6. Read the topic (first) sentence and the concluding (last) sentence of the paragraph. Write down the ideas that these two sentences have in common.

    _____

Example Paragraph 2

Taipei 101

I work in one of the world's tallest buildings—Taipei 101. This building is in Taipei's business **district**. Taipei 101 opened to the public in 2004. It is made of **steel** and glass panels, so it has a beautiful silver color. It has 101 **floors**. There are even five more levels below the building! Many international businesses have offices in Taipei 101. There are great places to shop in the building, too. I am **proud** to work in such an important place.

a district: an area

steel: a very strong metal

a floor: a level of a building

proud: having a very happy feeling of satisfaction

Post-Reading

1. How many sentences are in this paragraph? _____

2. What is the main topic of this paragraph? (Circle.)

    a. information about a city

    b. information about a person

    c. information about a building

3. What is the first sentence of this paragraph? (This is the topic sentence.) Write it here.

    _____

    _____

4. Answer these questions in complete sentences.

   a. Where is the building?

   _____

   b. How old is the building?

   _____

   c. What color is the building?

   _____

   d. How many floors does the building have in total?

   _____

5. Read the paragraph again. Find at least four adjectives and write them below.

   _____

6. Read the topic (first) sentence and the concluding (last) sentence of the paragraph. Write down the ideas that these two sentences have in common.

   _____

Parts of a Paragraph: The Topic Sentence

Every good paragraph has a **topic sentence**. The topic sentence is one sentence that tells the main idea of the whole paragraph.

The topic sentence:

- is usually the first sentence in the paragraph
- should not be too specific or too general
- must describe the information in all the sentences of the paragraph

If a paragraph does not have a topic sentence, the reader may be confused because the ideas will not be organized clearly. Make sure every paragraph has a topic sentence!

ACTIVITY 2 **Practicing Topic Sentences**

Read each paragraph and the three topic sentences below it. Choose the best topic sentence and write it on the lines. Then read the paragraph again. Make sure that the topic sentence gives the main idea for the whole paragraph. Remember to indent.

Beautiful Snow?

_____

_____ Snow is beautiful when it falls. After a few days, the snow is not beautiful anymore. It starts to **melt**, and the clean streets become **messy**. It is difficult to walk anywhere. The **sidewalks** are **slippery**. Snow also causes traffic problems. Some roads are closed. Other roads are **hard** to drive on safely. Drivers have more **accidents** on snowy roads. I understand why some people like snow, but I do not like it very much.

    a. In December, it usually snows.

    b. Some people like snow, but I do not.

    c. I love snow.

to melt: to change from ice to liquid

messy: sloppy; dirty

a sidewalk: a paved walkway on the side of roads

slippery: causing a person to slip or slide, usually because of a smooth surface

hard: difficult

an accident: a car crash

127

Maria and Her Great Job

_____ She works at Papa Joe's Restaurant. She **serves** about 60 people every day. Maria can remember all the dinner orders. If there is a problem with any of the food, she **takes** it **back** to the kitchen **immediately.** Maria works very hard to make sure all her customers have a great meal.

a. My cousin Maria is an excellent server.

b. My cousin Maria works at Papa Joe's Restaurant.

c. Maria's customers do not eat big meals.

to serve: to give someone food and drink at a restaurant

to take back: to return

immediately: at that moment; very quickly

My Favorite City

_____ I love to see all the interesting things there. The city is big, exciting, and full of life. I always visit the Statue of Liberty and the Empire State Building. I also visit Chinatown. At night, I go to **shows** on Broadway. The food in the city is excellent, too. I truly enjoy New York City.

a. I like to see the Statue of Liberty and the Empire State Building.

b. New York is a very big city.

c. My favorite city in the world is New York.

a show: a live performance on stage

Parts of a Paragraph: The Concluding Sentence

In addition to a topic sentence and body, every good paragraph has a **concluding sentence**. The concluding sentence ends the paragraph with a final thought.

The concluding sentence:

- often gives a summary of the information in the paragraph
- often gives information that is similar to the information in the topic sentence
- can be a **suggestion**, **opinion**, or **prediction**
- should <u>not</u> give any new information about the topic

ACTIVITY 3　Choosing Concluding Sentences

Read each paragraph and the three concluding sentences below it. Choose the best concluding sentence and write it on the lines. Then read the paragraph again. Make sure that the concluding sentence gives a final thought for the whole paragraph.

Example Paragraph 6

Monday

I hate Monday for many reasons. One reason is work. I get up early to go to work on Monday. After a weekend of fun and relaxation, I do not like to do this. Another reason that I do not like Monday is that I have three meetings every Monday. These meetings last a long time, and they are **extremely** boring. Traffic is also a big problem on Monday. There are more cars on the road on Monday. Drivers are in a bad **mood**, and I must be more careful than usual. _____

_____

extremely: very

a mood: a person's emotion at a particular time

    a. Monday is worse than Tuesday, but it is better than Sunday.

    b. I do not like meetings on Monday.

    c. These are just a few reasons why I do not like Monday.

Buying a Car

Buying a car **requires** careful planning. Do you want a new or a used car? This depends on how much money you can spend. Sometimes a used car needs repairs. What style of car do you want? You can look at many different models to help you decide. Next, do you want extra **features** in your new car? Adding lots of extra features makes a car more expensive. Finally, you have to decide where you will buy your car. _____

_____

to require: to need

a feature: an option, such as a DVD player or tinted windows

a. It is important to think about all of these things when you are buying a car.

b. The most important thing is the kind of car that you want to buy.

c. Will you buy your new car from a friend or a car dealer?

Hanami

Hanami is a very popular Japanese tradition. Every spring, thousands of **cherry** trees bloom all over Japan. For two weeks during Hanami, friends and families gather in parks and the countryside to see the beautiful flowers and celebrate the end of their vacation time. People make lots of food and have huge picnics under the lovely trees. There is lots of music and dancing, and large groups of people walk through the parks together. The celebration often continues into the night, and there are **lanterns** everywhere to light the celebration. _____

a cherry: a small red fruit

a lantern: a light with a decorative cover

a. People like to be with their family and friends during Hanami.

b. Looking at flowers during Hanami is interesting.

c. This is truly a most beloved Japanese custom.

Writing the English Alphabet

A a	B b	C c	D d	E e	F f	G g	H h	I i	J j
K k	L l	M m	N n	O o	P p	Q q	R r	S s	T t
U u	V v	W w	X x	Y y	Z z				

✓ There are 26 letters in the English alphabet.

    5 are vowels: A E I O U

    21 are consonants: B C D F G H J K L M N P Q R S T V W X Y Z

✓ When **w** and **y** come after a vowel, these two letters are silent vowels: **saw, grow, play, toy, buy.**

✓ When **w** and **y** are at the beginning of a syllable, they are consonant sounds: **wake, wish, when, year, young.**

Definitions of Useful Language Terms

Adjective   An adjective is a word that describes a noun.

Lexi is a very **smart** girl.

Adverb   An adverb is a word that describes a verb, an adjective, or another adverb.

The secretary types **quickly**. She types **very quickly**.

Article   The definite article is *the*. The indefinite articles are *a* and *an*.

The teacher gave **an** assignment to **the** students.
Jillian is eating **a** banana.

Clause   A clause is a group of words that has a subject-verb combination. Sentences can have one or more clauses.

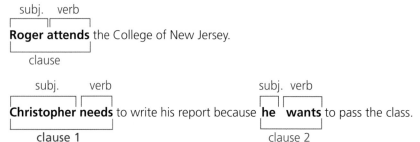

Noun   A noun is a person, place, thing, or idea.

Sandra likes to eat **sandwiches** for lunch.
Love is a very strong **emotion**.

Object   An object is a word that comes after a transitive verb or a preposition.

Jim bought a new **car**.
I left my **jacket** in the **house**.

Predicate   A predicate is the part of a sentence that shows what a subject does.

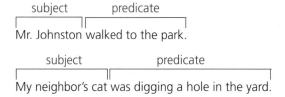

Preposition   A preposition is a word that can show location, time, and direction. Some common prepositions are *around, at, behind, between, from, on, in, near, to, over, under,* and *with*. Prepositions can also consist of two words (*next to*) or three words (*in addition to*).

Punctuation   Punctuation includes the period (.), comma (,), question mark (?), and exclamation point (!).

Subject   The subject of a sentence tells who or what the sentence is about.

My science teacher gave us a homework assignment. **It** was difficult.

Tense   A verb has tense. Tense shows when the action happened.

Simple Present: She **walks** to school every day.

Present Progressive: She **is walking** to school now.

Simple Past: She **walked** to school yesterday.

Past Progressive: She **was walking** to school when she saw her friend.

Simple Future: She **is going to walk** to school tomorrow.

Simple Future: She **will walk** to school tomorrow.

Verb   A verb is a word that shows the action of a sentence.

They **speak** French.

My father **works** at the power plant.

Review of Verb Tenses

Verb Tense	Affirmative	Negative	Usage
Simple Present	I work you take he studies she does we play they have	I do not work you do not take he does not study she does not do we do not play they do not have	• for routines, habits, and other actions that happen regularly • for facts and general truths
Simple Past	I worked you took he studied she did we played they had	I did not work you did not take he did not study she did not do we did not play they did not have	• for actions that were completed in the past
Present Progressive	I am working you are taking he is studying she is doing we are playing they are having*	I am not working you are not taking he is not studying she is not doing we are not playing they are not having*	• for actions that are happening now • for future actions if a future time adverb is used or understood
Simple Future (*Be Going To*)	I am going to work you are going to take he is going to study she is going to do we are going to play they are going to have	I am not going to work you are not going to take he is not going to study she is not going to do we are not going to play they are not going to have	• for plans that are already made • for predictions based on an action happening in the present
Simple Future (*Will*)	I will work you will take he will study she will do we will play they will have	I will not work you will not take he will not study she will not do we will not play they will not have	• for future plans or decisions that are made at the moment of speaking • for strong predictions • for promises/offers to help
Present Perfect	I have worked you have taken he has studied she has done we have played they have had	I have not worked you have not taken he has not studied she has not done we have not played they have not had	• for actions that began in the past and continue until the present • for actions in the indefinite past time • for repeated actions in the past
Past Progressive	I was working you were taking he was studying she was doing we were playing they were having*	I was not working you were not taking he was not studying she was not doing we were not playing they were not having*	• for longer actions in the past that are interrupted by other actions or events

Have can be used in progressive tenses only when it has an active meaning in special expressions, such as:

- *have* a party
- *have* a good time
- *have* a bad time
- *have* a baby

Capitalization Rules

1. The first word in a sentence is capitalized.

    I go to the movies every week.

    Deserts are beautiful places to visit.

2. The pronoun *I* is always capitalized.

    Larry and **I** are brothers.

3. People's formal and professional titles begin with capital letters.

    Mr. and **M**rs. Jenkins are on vacation.

    Lisa saw **D**r. Johansen at the bank yesterday.

4. Proper names (specific people and places) begin with capital letters.

    The **C**oliseum in **R**ome is a beautiful old monument.

    Kate met her brother **A**lex at the park.

5. Names of streets begin with capital letters.

    Ruth lives on **W**ilson **A**venue.

6. Geographical locations (cities, states, countries, continents, lakes, and rivers) begin with capital letters.

    I am going to travel to **L**ondon, **E**ngland, next week.

    The **A**rno **R**iver passes through **T**uscany, **I**taly.

7. The names of languages and nationalities begin with capital letters.

    My grandmother speaks **P**olish.

    Jessica is going to learn **J**apanese.

    Melissa is **V**enezuelan, but her husband is **C**uban.

8. Most words in titles of paragraphs, essays, and books are capitalized. The first letter of a title is always capitalized, and the other important words in a title are capitalized. Do not capitalize prepositions (*to, in*), conjunctions (*and, but*), or articles (*a, an, the*) unless they are the first word of the title.

    The Life of Billy Barnes

    Crime and Punishment

    The Catcher in the Rye

    In the Bedroom

9. Specific course names are capitalized.

    Nick is taking **H**istory 101 at 10:00 A.M.

    Nick is taking history this semester. (general subject—no capital letter)

Eight Common Comma Rules

1. Put a comma before *and, but, for, or, nor, so,* and *yet* when they connect two simple sentences. This creates a compound sentence.

    Rick bought Julia a croissant**,** but he ate it himself.

2. Put a comma between three or more items in a list or series.

    Jen brought a towel**,** an umbrella**,** some sunscreen**,** and a book to the beach.

3. Put a comma after a dependent clause (a clause that begins with a connecting word) when that clause begins a sentence. This is called a complex sentence.

> Because it was raining outside, Alex used his umbrella.

4. Put a comma before or after the name of a person spoken to.

> "Hamad, do you want to play soccer?" Ana asked.
>
> "Do you want to play soccer, Hamad?" Ana asked.

5. Commas separate parts of dates and places. Put a comma between the day and the date. Put a comma between the date and the year. Put a comma between a city and a state or a country. Put an additional comma after the state or country name if it appears in the middle of a sentence.

> I was born on Tuesday, June 27, 1992.
>
> The concert was in Busan, Korea.
>
> The headquarters of that company is located in Osaka, Japan.
>
> I lived in Phuket, Thailand, for ten years.

6. Use a comma to separate an introductory word or phrase from the rest of the sentence.

> Finally, they decided to ask the police for help.
>
> Every afternoon after school, I go to the library.

NOTE: *Then* is not followed by a comma.

7. Use a comma to separate information that is not necessary in a sentence.

> Rome, which is the capital of Italy, has a lot of pollution.
>
> George Washington, the first president of the United States, was a military officer.

8. Put a comma after the salutation in personal letters and after the closing in personal and business letters.

> Dear Roberta,   Dear Dr. Gomez,   Dear Ms. Kennedy,
>
> With love,   Sincerely,   Yours truly,
>   Grandma   Jonathan   Alicia

Spelling Rules for Regular Simple Present Verbs and Plural Nouns

1. Add -s to the base form of most verbs and to most nouns.

run	runs
work	works
love	loves

2. If a verb/noun ends in an *x*, *z*, *s*, *sh*, or *ch*, add -es.

box	boxes
buzz	buzzes
pass	passes
push	pushes
watch	watches

3. If a verb/noun ends in a consonant + *y*, change the *y* to *i* and add -es.

carry	carries
worry	worries
party	parties

4. If a verb/noun ends in a vowel + *y*, add -*s*. Do not change the *y*.

pay	pays
boy	boys
destroy	destroys

5. Add -*es* to *go* and *do.*

go	goes
do	does

Spelling Rules for Regular Simple Past Tense Verbs

1. Add -*ed* to the base form of most verbs.

start	started
finish	finished
wash	washed

2. Add only -*d* when the base form ends in an *e*.

live	lived
care	cared
die	died

3. If a verb ends in a consonant + *y*, change the *y* to *i* and add -*ed*.

dry	dried
carry	carried
study	studied

4. If a verb ends in a vowel + *y*, do not change the *y*. Just add -*ed*.

play	played
stay	stayed
destroy	destroyed

5. If a verb has one syllable and ends in a consonant + vowel + consonant (CVC), double the final consonant and add -*ed.*

stop	sto**pp**ed
CVC	
rob	ro**bb**ed
CVC	

6. If a verb ends in a *w* or *x,* do not double the final consonant. Just add -*ed.*

sew	sewed
mix	mixed

7. If a verb that ends in CVC has two syllables and the <u>second</u> syllable is stressed, double the final consonant and add -*ed.*

ad mit'	admi**tt**ed
oc cur'	occu**rr**ed
per mit'	permi**tt**ed

8. If a verb that ends in CVC has two syllables and the <u>first</u> syllable is stressed, do *not* double the final consonant. Just add -*ed.*

hap' pen	happe**n**ed
lis' ten	liste**n**ed
o' pen	ope**n**ed

Irregular Simple Past Tense Verbs

These are some of the more common irregular verbs in English.

Base Form	Simple Past
be (am/is/are)	was/were
become	became
begin	began
bite	bit
bleed	bled
blow	blew
break	broke
bring	brought
build	built
buy	bought
catch	caught
choose	chose
come	came
cost	cost
cut	cut
do	did
draw	drew
drink	drank
drive	drove
eat	ate
fall	fell
feel	felt
fight	fought
find	found
flee	fled
forget	forgot
get	got
give	gave
grow	grew
have	had
hear	heard
hide	hid
hit	hit
hold	held

Base Form	Simple Past
hurt	hurt
keep	kept
know	knew
leave	left
let	let
lose	lost
make	made
pay	paid
put	put
read	read
run	ran
say	said
see	saw
sell	sold
send	sent
set	set
sing	sang
sink	sank
sit	sat
sleep	slept
speak	spoke
spend	spent
stand	stood
steal	stole
swim	swam
take	took
teach	taught
tell	told
think	thought
throw	threw
understand	understood
wear	wore
win	won
write	wrote

Possessive Pronouns

In general, possessive pronouns are used in spoken English. However, it is important to know how to use them. Possessive pronouns take the place of a possessive adjective + noun combination. In a sentence, a possessive pronoun can be a subject or an object.

Possessive Pronoun	Example
mine	That is not your book. It is **mine** (= my book).
yours (singular)	I don't have my pencil. I need to use **yours** (= your book).
his	My ring is silver, but **his** (= his ring) is gold.
hers	Carol has my cell phone, and I have **hers** (= her cell phone).
ours	Your room is on the first floor. **Ours** (= our room) is on the fifth floor.
yours (plural)	Our class got to have a special party. **Yours** (= your class) did not.
theirs	Jenny likes her class, and Karl and Jim like **theirs** (= their class), too.

Order of Adjectives

Adjectives can go before nouns. When more than one adjective is used before a noun, there is a certain order for the adjectives.

Example: He has a **brown** dog. It is an **enormous** dog.

✗ He has a brown enormous dog.

✓ He has an enormous brown dog.

In general, there are seven kinds of adjectives. They are used in this order:

1. size   *small, large, huge*

2. opinion   *beautiful, nice, ugly*

3. shape   *round, square, oval*

4. condition   *broken, damaged, burned*

5. age   *old, young, new*

6. color   *red, white, green*

7. origin   *French, American, Korean*

It is common to have two adjectives before a noun but rare to have three or more adjectives before a noun. When there is more than one adjective before a noun, follow the order above. The noun always goes last. Remember that this list is only a general guideline.

✗ a white Japanese small truck

✓ a small white Japanese truck

✗ a broken large dish

✓ a large broken dish

Quantifiers

Quantifiers give more information about the quantity, or number, of a noun. Quantifiers usually go in front of a noun.

Quantifier	Example
With Count Nouns	
one, two, three (all numbers) a few few many another several a pair of a couple of	**Several** students went to the school office. **Many** people wanted to leave the city. Ellie put **a few** coins in the parking meter.
With Non-count Nouns	
a little little much	There is only a **little** milk left in the refrigerator. We get too **much** homework every night.
With Count or Non-count Nouns	
some (quantity meaning *only*) any a lot of the other other	They got into **a lot of** trouble. Mrs. Jones has **a lot of** friends. Adam does not have **any** money.

The Prepositions *At, On,* and *In*

Prepositions express different ideas. They can indicate time, location, and direction. Remember that a preposition is usually followed by a noun (or pronoun).

Three very common prepositions in English are *at, on,* and *in*. In general, we use *at* with small, specific times and places, *on* with middle-sized times and places, and *in* with larger, more general times and places.

	Time	Place
Small	**at** 1:00 P.M.	**at** the bus stop
Middle	**on** Monday	**on** Bayview Avenue
Large	**in** July **in** spring **in** 2004 **in** this century	**in** Toronto **in** Ontario **in** Canada **in** North America

The Preposition *At*

Location: Use *at* for specific locations.

Angela works **at** the First National Bank.

I always do my homework **at** my desk.

Joel met Jillian **at** the corner of Polk Street and Florida Avenue.

Time: Use *at* for specific times.

My grammar class meets **at** 9:00 A.M. every day.

The lunch meeting begins **at** noon.

Cate does not like to walk alone **at** night.

Direction: Use *at* for motion toward a goal.

My brother threw a ball **at** me.

The robber pointed his gun **at** the policewoman.

The Preposition *On*

Location: Use *on* when there is contact between two objects. We also use *on* with streets.

The picture is **on** the wall.

He put his books **on** the kitchen table.

Erin lives **on** Bayshore Boulevard.

Time: Use *on* with specific days or dates.

Our soccer game is **on** Saturday.

Your dentist appointment is **on** October 14.

I was born **on** June 22, 1988.

The Preposition *In*

Location: Use *in* when something is inside another thing.

The books are **in** the big box.

I left my jacket **in** your car.

Barbara lives **in** Istanbul.

Time: Use *in* for a specific period of time, a specific year, or a future time.

I am going to graduate from college **in** three years.

My best friend got married **in** 2006.

Mr. Johnson always drinks four cups of coffee **in** the morning.

We will meet you **in** ten minutes.

More Prepositions

Here are a few more common prepositions of location. Remember that a preposition is usually followed by a noun (or pronoun). In the chart, the preposition shows the location of the ball (in relation to the box).

Preposition	Example
in	The gift is **in** the box.
on	Marta's gift is **on** the table.
under	Pedro keeps his shoes **under** his bed.
above/over	Sheila held the umbrella **over** her head to stay dry.
between	The milk is **between** the eggs and the butter.
in front of	Mark was standing in **front of** the restaurant.
in back of/behind	My shirt fell **behind** my dresser.
across...from	There is a supermarket **across** the street **from** my house.
next to/beside	The mailman left the package **next to** the door.

Useful Connectors for Writing

Coordinating Conjunctions

Coordinating conjunctions are used to connect two independent clauses (sentences).

Note: A comma usually appears before a coordinating conjunction that separates two independent clauses. (An exception is when the two clauses are both very short.)

Purpose	Coordinating Conjunction	Example
To show reason	**for***	He ate a sandwich, **for** he was hungry.
To add information	**and**	Carla lives in Toronto, **and** she is a student.
To add negative information	**nor****	Roberto does not like opera, **nor** does he enjoy hip-hop.
To show contrast	**but**†	The exam was difficult, **but** everyone passed.
To give a choice	**or**	We can eat Chinese food, **or** we can order a pizza.
To show concession/contrast	**yet**†	The exam was difficult, **yet** everyone passed.
To show result	**so**	It was raining, **so** we decided to stay home last night.

*The conjunction **for** is not common in English. It may be used in literary writing, but it is almost never used in spoken English.

Notice that question word order is used in the clause that follows **nor.

†The conjunctions **but** and **yet** have similar meanings. However, **yet** is generally used to show a stronger contrast.

Many writers remember these conjunctions with the acronym **FANBOYS**. Each letter represents one conjunction: **F = for**, **A = and**, **N = nor**, **B = but**, **O = or**, **Y = yet**, and **S = so**.

Subordinating Conjunctions

Subordinating conjunctions are used to connect a dependent clause and an independent clause.

NOTE: When the sentence begins with the dependent clause, a comma should be used after that clause.

Purpose	Subordinating Conjunction	Example
To show reason/cause	because	He ate a sandwich **because** he was hungry.
	since	**Since** he was hungry, he ate a sandwich.
	as	**As** he was hungry, he ate a sandwich.
To show contrast	although	**Although** the exam was difficult, everyone passed.
	even though	**Even though** the exam was difficult, everyone passed.
	though	**Though** the exam was difficult, everyone passed.
	while	Deborah is a dentist **while** John is a doctor.
To show time relationship	after	**After** we ate dinner, we went to a movie.
	before	We ate dinner **before** we went to a movie.
	until	I will not call you **until** I finish studying.
	while	**While** the pasta is cooking, I will cut the vegetables.
	as	**As** I was leaving the office, it started to rain.
To show condition	if	**If** it rains tomorrow, we will stay home.
	even if	We will go to the park **even if** it rains tomorrow.

Useful Vocabulary for Better Writing

Try these useful words and phrases as you write your sentences and paragraphs. They can make your writing sound more academic, natural, and fluent.

Topic Sentences

Words and phrases	Examples
There are QUANTIFIER (ADJECTIVE) SUBJECT…	*There are* many good places to visit in my country.
SUBJECT *must follow* QUANTIFIER (ADJECTIVE) *steps to* VERB…	A tourist *must follow* several simple *steps to* get a visa to visit my country.
There are QUANTIFIER (ADJECTIVE) *types / methods / ways*…	*There are* three different *types* of runners.
It is ADJECTIVE *to* VERB…	*It is* easy *to* make ceviche.

Supporting Sentence Markers

Words and phrases	Examples
One NOUN…	*One* reason to visit my country is the wonderful weather.
Another NOUN… … *another* NOUN	*Another* reason to visit my country is the delicious food. The delicious food is *another* reason to visit my country.
The first / second / next / final NOUN…	*The final* reason to visit my country is its wonderful people.

Giving and Adding Examples

Words and phrases	Examples
For example, S + V. *For instance,* S + V.	My instructor gives us so much homework. *For example,* yesterday he gave us five pages of grammar work.

Concluding Sentences

Words and phrases	Examples
In conclusion, S + V.	*In conclusion,* I believe that my parents are the best in the world.
It is clear that S + V.	*It is clear that* Guatemala is the best tourist destination in South America.
If you follow these important steps in VERB + *-ING*…, S + V.	*If you follow these important steps in* fixing a computer, you will not need to call an expert.

Telling a Story

Words and phrases	Examples
When I was X, *I would* VERB…	*When I was* a teenager, *I would* go to the beach with my friends every day.
When I think about that time, S + V.	*When I think about that time*, I remember my grandparents' love for me.
I will never forget NOUN…	*I will never forget* the day I left my country.
I can still remember NOUN… *I will always remember* NOUN…	*I can still remember* the day I started my first job.
X *was the best / worst day of my life.*	My sixteenth birthday *was the best day of my life.*
Every time S +V, S + V.	*Every time* I tried to speak English, my tongue refused to work!

Describing a Process

Words and phrases	Examples
First (*Second, Third*, etc.), *Next*, … / *After that*, … / *Then* … *Finally*, …	*First*, you cut the fish and vegetables into small pieces. *Next*, you add the lime juice. *After that*, you add in the seasonings. *Finally*, you mix everything together well.
The first thing you should do is VERB…	*The first thing you should do is* wash your hands.
Before S + V, S + V.	*Before* you cut up the vegetables, you need to wash them.
After / When S + V, S + V. *After that*, S + V.	*After* you cut up the vegetables, you need to add them to the salad. *After that*, you need to mix the ingredients.
The last / final step is… *Finally*, …	*The last step is* adding your favorite salad dressing. *Finally*, you should add your favorite salad dressing.

Showing Cause and Effect

Words and phrases	Examples
Because S+ V, S + V. S + V *because* S + V. *Because of* NOUN, S + V. S + V *because of* NOUN.	*Because* I broke my leg, I could not move. I could not move *because* I broke my leg. *Because of* my broken leg, I could not move. I could not move *because of* my broken leg.
CAUSE, *so* RESULT.	My sister did not know what to do, *so* she asked my mother for advice.

Describing

Words and phrases	Examples
Prepositions of location: *above, across, around, in, near, under*…	The children raced their bikes *around* the school.
Descriptive adjectives: *wonderful, delightful, dangerous, informative, rusty*…	The *bent, rusty* bike squeaked when I rode it.
SUBJECT + *BE* + ADJECTIVE.	The Terra Cotta Warriors of Xian *are amazing.*
SUBJECT + *BE* + *the most* ADJECTIVE + NOUN.	To me, Thailand *is the most* interesting country in the world.
SUBJECT *tastes / looks / smells / feels like* NOUN.	My ID card *looks like* a credit card.

SUBJECT + *BE* + *known* / *famous for its* NOUN.	France *is famous for its* cheese.
Adverbs of manner: *quickly, slowly, quietly, happily…*	I *quickly* wrote his phone number on a scrap of paper that I found on the table.

Stating an Opinion

Words and phrases	Examples
Personally, I believe / think / feel / agree / disagree / suppose (*that*) S + V.	*Personally, I believe that* New York City should ban large sugary drinks.
VERB + *-ING should not be allowed.*	*Smoking* in public *should not be allowed.*
In my opinion / view / experience, S + V.	*In my opinion,* smoking is rude.
For this reason, S + V. *That is why I think that* S + V.	*That is why I think that* smoking should not be allowed in restaurants.
There are many benefits / advantages to VERB + *-ING.*	*There are many benefits to* swimming every day.
There are many drawbacks / disadvantages to VERB + *-ING.*	*There are many drawbacks to* eating most of your meals at a restaurant.
I prefer X [NOUN] *to* Y [NOUN].	*I prefer* soccer *to* football.
To me, VERB + *-ING makes* (*perfect*) *sense.*	*To me,* exercising every day *makes perfect sense.*
For all of these important reasons, I think / believe (*that*) S + V.	*For all of these important reasons, I think* smoking is bad for your health.

Arguing and Persuading

Words and phrases	Examples
It is important to remember that S+V.	*It is important to remember that* students only wear their uniforms during school hours.
According to a recent survey / poll, S + V.	*According to a recent poll,* 85 percent of high school students felt they had too much homework.
Even more important, S + V.	*Even more important,* statistics show the positive effects of school uniforms on student behavior.
SUBJECT *must / should / ought to* VERB.	Researchers *must* stop unethical animal testing.
I agree that S + V. *However,* S + V.	*I agree that* eating healthily is important. *However,* the government should not make food choices for us.

Reacting/Responding

Words and phrases	Examples
TITLE *by* AUTHOR *is a / an* (ADJECTIVE) NOUN.	*Harry Potter and the Goblet of Fire by* J.K. Rowling *is an* entertaining book to read.
My first reaction to the prompt / news / article / question was / is NOUN.	*My first reaction to the article was* anger.
When I read / looked at / thought about NOUN, *I was amazed / shocked / surprised…*	*When I read* the article, *I was surprised* to learn of his athletic ability.

Building Better Sentences

Being a good writer involves many skills including correct grammar usage, varied vocabulary, and conciseness (avoiding unnecessary words). Some student writers like to keep their sentences simple. They feel that they will make mistakes if they write longer, more complicated sentences. However, writing short, choppy sentences one after the other is not considered appropriate in academic writing. Study the examples below.

> The time was yesterday.
>
> It was afternoon.
>
> There was a storm.
>
> The storm was strong.
>
> The movement of the storm was quick.
>
> The storm moved towards the coast.
>
> The coast was in North Carolina.

Notice that every sentence has an important piece of information. A good writer would not write all these sentences separately. Instead, the most important information from each sentence can be used to create ONE longer, coherent sentence.

Read the sentences again; this time, the important information has been circled.

> The time was (yesterday.)
>
> It was (afternoon.)
>
> There was a (storm.)
>
> The storm was (strong.)
>
> The (movement) of the storm was (quick.)
>
> The storm (moved towards the coast.)
>
> The coast was in (North Carolina.)

Here are some strategies for taking the circled information and creating a new sentence.

1. Create time phrases to begin or end a sentence: yesterday + afternoon
2. Find the key noun: storm
3. Find key adjectives: strong
4. Create noun phrases: a strong + storm
5. Change word forms: movement = move; quick = quickly
   moved + quickly
6. Create place phrases: towards the coast

   towards the coast (of North Carolina)

   or

   towards the North Carolina coast

Better Sentence:

Yesterday afternoon, a strong storm moved quickly towards the North Carolina coast.

Here are some other strategies for building better sentences.

7. Use connectors and transition words.

8. Use pronouns to replace frequently used nouns.

9. Use possessive adjectives and pronouns.

Study the following example:

(Susan) (went) somewhere. That place was (the mall.) Susan wanted to (buy new shoes.) The shoes were for (Susan's mother.)

Improved, Longer Sentence:

Susan went to the mall because she wanted to buy new shoes for her mother.

Practices

Follow these steps for each practice:

Step 1: Read the sentences. Circle the most important information in each sentence.

Step 2: Write an original sentence from the information you circled. Remember that there is more than one way to combine sentences.

Practice 1

A. 1. (Tina) is my (friend.)

2. Tina (works.)

3. The work is at (Washington Central Bank.)

_____ My friend Tina works at Washington Central Bank. _____

_____

B. 1. There are boxes.

2. The boxes are on the table.

3. The boxes are heavy.

_____

_____

C. 1. Caroline attends classes.

2. The classes are at Jefferson Community College.

3. The classes are on Wednesdays.

_____

_____

D. 1. Tuscany is a region.

2. This region is in Italy.

3. This region is beautiful.

_____

_____

Practice 2

A. 1. There are books.

   2. The books are rare.

   3. The books are in the library.

_____

_____

B. 1. Drivers have more accidents.

   2. The accidents happen on roads.

   3. The roads are snowy.

_____

_____

C. 1. Aspirin is good for headaches.

   2. Aspirin is good for colds.

   3. Aspirin is good for pain.

_____

_____

Practice 3

A. 1. Charlie is a man.

   2. Charlie is my uncle.

   3. Charlie works hard in a restaurant.

   4. The restaurant belongs to Charlie.

_____

_____

B. 1. Tourists often ride boats.

   2. The boats are on the Seine River.

   3. Tourists do this at night.

   4. Tourists do this to see the Eiffel Tower's lights.

   5. The tower's lights are beautiful.

_____

_____

C. 1. Steven is in bed.

    2. It is early.

    3. Steven does this to be ready to work hard.

    4. He is doing this again.

    5. His work is the next day.

_____

_____

Practice 4

A. (Hint: Use a coordinating conjunction.)

    1. Chavez's family received money.

    2. There was very little money.

    3. People treated them badly.

_____

_____

B. (Hint: Use a coordinating conjunction.)

    1. My parents were not rich.

    2. My parents were always happy.

_____

_____

C. 1. This book gives us information.

    2. There is a lot of information.

    3. The book gives us the information now.

    4. The information is important.

    5. The information is about life in the fourteenth century.

_____

_____

Practice 5

A. (Hint: Use a coordinating conjunction.)

    1. Angela needs to buy some fruits.

    2. Angela needs to buy some vegetables.

    3. Angela is shopping at the farmer's market.

_____

_____

B. 1. Visitors are standing in line.

    2. There are many visitors.

    3. The visitors are also waiting to take pictures.

    4. The pictures are of themselves.

    5. There are ruins in the background.

_____

_____

C. (Hint: Use a coordinating conjunction.)

    1. Lisana is working.

    2. This company works with computers.

    3. Lisana does not have a computer engineering degree.

_____

_____

Practice 6

A. (HINT: Create a complex sentence.)

    1. First, Carmen arrives.

    2. Then Carmen will perform some dances.

    3. These dances will be formal.

    4. Carmen will do these dances with her friends.

_____

_____

B. (HINT: Create a complex sentence.)

    1. I go to the theater.

    2. The theater is on Broadway.

    3. I do this often.

    4. The reason I do this is that I live in New York.

_____

_____

C. (HINT: Create a complex sentence.)

   1. First, I will arrive in Canada.

   2. Next, I am going to buy a lot of souvenirs.

   3. There will be souvenirs for my parents.

   4. There will be souvenirs for my brother.

   5. There will be souvenirs for my friends.

_____

_____

Practice 7

A. (HINT: Use an adjective clause.)

   1. The two women are my grandmother and my mother.

   2. The women are sitting on the sofa.

_____

_____

B. (HINT: Use an adjective clause.)

   1. These are words.

   2. There are just a few of these words.

   3. These words cause problems for English speakers.

   4. These problems are with spelling.

   5. These speakers are native and nonnative.

_____

_____

C. 1. Jenna is eating lunch.

   2. Jenna is talking to her friends.

   3. Jenna is in the cafeteria.

   4. Jenna is doing these things right now.

_____

_____

NOTES

NOTES

NOTES